SELMA

The Other Side of 1965

by

The Reverend P. H. Lewis

FACTOR PRESS
Post Office Box 8888
Mobile, Alabama 36689
2001

Publisher's Cataloging-in-Publication Data
Lewis, P.H.
SELMA, the other side of 1965/P.H. Lewis.
213p.22.86cm.
ISBN 1-0887650-34-2
1. Civil rights movements—Alabama—Selma—20th century.
2. Selma (Ala)—Race relations.
3. Civil rights—Religious aspects—African Methodist Episcopal Church
I. Title
E185.61 .L49 2001

Typesetting by Curious Cat Productions

DEDICATION

To Mother and Father,
Ben and Daisy Lewis, who are looking down from glory
my Sisters and Brothers
my wife Mrs. Alice P. G. Lewis
my son Prinic Lewis Jr.: Sons Kenneth Lewis and wife
Kimberly, Bernard Howard and wife Alberta,
my grandchildren: Kameron Lewis, Alex Lewis, Derice
Lewis, and Brittany Howard.

I also dedicate this book to my Bethel A.M.E. Church Family.

ACKNOWLEDGMENTS

I wish to express my thanks to Mrs. Margaret Johnson, Ms. Mary Weatherspoon, Mrs. Marva Rodrigues, Rev. Cortia Chandler, Mrs. Vernetta Greene, Charles and Perri Grady, Clifford Grady, Gail Lewis, Daisy Lewis, and Mrs. Carolyn Oliver for typing and reading the material.

CONTENTS

FORWARD

WHAT IF?

In retrospect, what if Richard Allen and the others that followed him when he walked out of St. George's Methodist Church of Philadelphia in 1787 and started the African Methodist Episcopal Church, would have gone to the balcony as the white church elders told them to do? Just maybe black folks would still be in the balconies of every white church in America. But they left as a protest for human dignity and self-respect.

That has been more than two hundred and fourteen years ago. This Church in its history has elected one hundred and nineteen bishops; nineteen active now, two located, four retired; many, many general officers, hundreds of presiding elders, thousands of pastors and over a million lay members. The Church has as its Motto: "God Our Father, Christ Our Redeemer, Man our Brother, regardless of race, creed, or national origin."

When I look at our rich history in the many schools that have been established to help mold and shape our people into Christian men and women, boys and girls, I wonder sometimes where

7

would we be if there were no Christian schools? It is bad enough as it is. So, just think where we would be as a people if Richard Allen had gone into the balcony that dreadful day. Just maybe we would still be sitting there, but instead we are on the road to freedom.

What if Mrs. Rosa Parks had decided to give up her seat to a white man in 1955? Perhaps we would still be riding in the back of the buses only. Three other black folks got up and moved to the back when the bus driver asked them to move. But Mrs. Rosa Parks refused to give up her seat. Just think how far it would set black folks back had she decided to move to the back of the bus. Maybe black folks would still be riding in the back of the buses in 2001. But because of the raw courage that Mrs. Rosa Parks exemplified on that day in 1955, it has not been the same when it comes to black folks riding the buses. Their theme then was "walk in dignity, rather than ride in shame." The people "walked in dignity" for more than three hundred days, or until the court declared that segregation on public buses was unconstitutional. Black folks would never have gotten this answer if Mrs. Rosa Parks had not refused to move from her seat. Of course you know and I know that was her seat. She paid the fare to ride the bus just like the white man, so why should she have to move? In point of fact, if he had been a gentleman, he would have given her his seat.

Behind every great invention stands an individual and behind every great movement stands an individual. Behind the bus boycott in Montgomery, Alabama, in 1955 without a shadow of doubt is Mrs. Rosa Parks.

I got a peculiar feeling when my wife and I went to Memphis, Tennessee, last August and visited the old Lorraine Motel, which has been turned into a Civil Rights museum. We saw among many things the bus that Mrs. Parks was riding on that day. They have a bust of the bus driver seated in the driver's seat and a bust of Mrs. Parks sitting in that same seat she was in that day. When you step up on the bus, there is a recording of the bus driver saying, "Get out of that seat! I need that seat. If you don't move I will have you arrested." Mrs. Parks never said anything, but just sat there until she was arrested. What a great spirit she has!

Historic Brown Chapel A.M.E. Church, 410 Martin Luther King Jr. Street, Selma, Alabama. During the sixties, the church became known throughout the world as the headquarters for the voting rights movement. This was during the pastorate of the Reverend P.H. Lewis. The church was the starting point for the marchers on the Selma to Montgomery march.

What if Reverend P. H. Lewis had not opened the doors of Brown Chapel African Methodist Episcopal Church in 1965, when Judge James Hare issued his infamous injunction prohibiting more than three persons to meet to discuss the 1964 Civil Right Bill? To violate this injunction carried a fine and a jail term. Other ministers were asked to open their doors, but they refused. They needed a place to meet on January 2, 1965, for Emancipation services, because they had invited Dr. Martin Luther King Jr. as the main speaker. In spite of the injunction, in spite of what might have happened to my family and in spite of what might have happened to me, I took the risk and opened the doors to the church. They stayed opened 24/7, until we won the 1965 Voting Rights Bill. I often wonder what would have happened if l had not opened the doors. We might be still paying poll taxes, trying to fill out that old literacy test, et cetera, with the registrar's office opening two days a month. Opening at 9 a.m., closing at 11 a.m., three hours for lunch. Opening from 2 p.m. to 4 p.m., closing for the day. The board might have registered four or five people that day. There were more than thirteen thousand Blacks that needed to be registered, but at the rate the Board was going it would have taken them three or four hundred years just to register eligible Blacks. We couldn't wait that long, so it was important that I open the doors of the church for the movement. One act like this injunction, issued by Judge James Hare, can set black folks back for years, and it does not have to be legal in order for it to be effective. This injunction was definitely unconstitutional. Observe the following:

STATE CONSTITUTIONS

Each State Constitution contains a Bill of Rights or a declaration of rights. It guarantees the fundamentals listed in the United States Constitution.

10

AMENDMENT I

"Congress shall make no law respecting establishment of religion, or prohibiting the free exercise thereof or abridging the freedom of speech, or of the press; or the rights of the people peaceably to assemble, and to petition the government for a redress of grievances."

This Amendment speaks specifically against the very injunction issued by Judge James Hare in July of 1965 prohibiting anyone to peacefully assemble. It was a violation of the Constitution of the United States and a violation of our constitutional rights. One cannot believe that Judge Hare did not know the law, but, as so many others have done in the Deep South, he tried to circumvent the law of the land and substitute custom and tradition. Maybe there was a time when custom and tradition worked in favor of the South, but to the white man's surprise there is a new Negro who discovered that custom and tradition have kept the Negro in "his place" too long. Yes, too long have we been the last hired and the first fired. Too long have we lived on unpaved and dark streets. Too long have we lived in the ghettos that the politicians and the greedy businessmen have made larger, and the exit smaller. Too long now, although we are a minority in this country, have we had a majority of our black boys in prison. Too long have we been governed by custom and tradition.

Where is justice when it comes to the black man? Justice seems to be blind when it comes to dealing with African Americans. The scales of justice always seem to be out of balance when it comes to people of color. The old cliché goes, *"If you are white you are right, if you are yellow, you are mellow, if you are brown stick around, but if you are black, get back."*

White is not always right. Cases in point are the infamous injunction issued by Judge James Hare and many other such cases too numerous to mention. If you are "yellow you are mellow," Mellow means too ripe. If you are "brown stick around." They will stick around through thick and thin and when it gets too thick, then they will thin out. If you are "black, get back." I believe that our track record will make clear that black folks have never gotten back in spite of the situation or the circumstances. The slaves never accepted slavery—otherwise, why did so many of them run away? Black folks were not satisfied with segregated schools that said separate but equal; always separate but never equal, until the 1954 Supreme Court decision, making "separate but equal" unconstitutional. The mere fact that black folks were never satisfied with slavery, separate but equal, customs, tradition, et cetera, is our way of saying, black folks don't play "get back." Our motto is, "Forward ever and backward never."

I

THE MOVEMENT

COME ONE! COME ALL!

TO AN EMANCIPATION MEETING

HELD AT

BROWN CHAPEL AFRICAN METHODIST
EPISCOPAL CHURCH

REV. P. H. LEWIS, PASTOR!

SATURDAY, JANUARY 2, 1965 AT
4:00 P.M.

MAIN SPEAKER

DR. MARTIN LUTHER KING, JR.

WE NEED EACH OTHER

The Man Who Thinks He Can Go It Alone . . . Is Worse
Off Than Sheep Without a Shepherd.

Together We Can Motivate While We Choose To
Emancipate Our People And Liberate Our People
Who Are Denied The RIGHT TO VOTE

After the January 2, 1965, meeting, it was time to go to work on implementing plans to get Negroes the right to vote in masses. SCLC and SNCC field workers had been in Selma and Dallas county for months trying to condition the people to the idea of becoming first class citizens by becoming registered voters. As things stood, Negroes were suffering taxation without representation. All citizens were required to pay tax, but we were prohibited from becoming registered voters by various methods by the "powers that be." At times we didn't know what to do, but our situation and circumstances told us we needed to do something, even if it was wrong. The leaders of the Dallas County Voter's League, Southern Christian Leadership Conference, and the Student Nonviolence Coordinating Committee felt that the season was right, the people were ready to face risk in order to gain their freedom. We recognized the old saying, "Nothing ventured, nothing gained." We as Christians didn't expect the road to be easy; some folks burned crosses, but we have learned to *bear* crosses. So, we were willing to bear the cross down to the courthouse or to the Statehouse.

We first checked to see what days the registrar's office was opened. The day we discovered it was open, we organized to march down there. That was a happy day, to see all the local people in line, led by Dr. King and the rest of the local leaders. We prayed before we left the church and when we got midway there we prayed again, because we didn't know what might happen to the marchers. We were told by Wilson Baker, the city's Public Safety Director, that we couldn't march because we did not have a permit. But Dr. King said to him, "Oh, yes, we are going to march down to the courthouse to register to vote, because the first Amendment gives us the right of peaceful assembly." Upon hearing that, Wilson Baker said, "You may march, but you must obey all traffic signs." We marched two across and obeyed all traffic signs.

When we reached the courthouse, instead of being able to get in, we were met by Sheriff Jim Clark and his deputies. They barred the door, preventing us from entering. Sheriff Jim Clark took charge after we arrived at the steps of the courthouse. It was a tense moment for a while; you would have thought that we had broken some law, just for coming to the courthouse, when all we wanted was to be allowed to register to vote. That was the only thing on our agenda, but it appeared that they had another agenda.

We were called agitators. One definition of an agitator is "to stir people up for social and political change." Lord knows we needed a change as bad as a dead person needed a casket. We wanted to and did "stir up" the non-violent way. We had nothing to offer but our bodies and souls in exchange for our freedom. The "powers that be" had all the weapons and the authority to use them. But we were willing to risk it all for the cause of justice and righteousness. When Jim Clark used to call Dr. King an "agitator" King would say, "My mother once had a washing machine that had an agitator in it, and oh, how it would clean the dirt from the clothes." In a way that's what the civil rights workers were all about, cleaning up the Board of Registrars, so it would do away with the literacy test that consisted of one hundred questions. I'm not talking about what somebody told me or something I read about. The literacy test was something I saw with my own eyes, felt in my hands, tried to fill out, but couldn't.

We wanted to clean up county and city government, so that Negroes who worked for the county as day laborers would be paid fair and just wages along with benefits. It has been alleged that the Negro county workers were paid a flat fifty dollars per week, rain or shine, with no benefits. The "agitators" cleaned this up.

The "agitators" had to clean up city government, because everything was "lily white." The City Council consisted of eleven people, all of them white. The county Commissioners consisted of three, all of them white. All policemen were white, the Sheriff and all of his deputies were white, and the Board of Registrars were all white. One would think that there were no Negroes living in the city or county. Yet Negroes constituted more than fifty-one percent of the county population. We needed some "agitators" to stir up the Negroes from apathy and complacency to equality and dignity and to clean up the city and county of its all-whiteness.

We spent a great deal of time on that first march down to our courthouse; I said "our" courthouse because we were tax payers and that made it ours too. The word was passed on back to those in line to return to the church in the same manner in which we came down. After we got back to the church, Dr. King and the leaders made their assessment of the march and began to plan our next move. Many suggestions were made and we narrowed them down, deciding to march again to the courthouse and stay until we got arrested.

The next time we marched, the people were there. I mean local people in the city of Selma and the County of Dallas. They were there ready to march, go to jail, and die if need be. That's why I called them "members of the ground crew." There were different groups, all fighting for the same cause. There were people from all walks of life, but we at this point were all on the same page. There were more than fifty preachers in line ready to march and go to jail. There were professional teachers in line ready to lose their jobs, ready to march and to go to jail; there were elderly people in line ready to march and to go to jail; there were the domestic workers in line, who were not afraid that their bosses would see them, in line marching for first-class citizenship; and then there were our young people, full of energy, ready to sing, march and go to jail.

What a joy it was to see this group of dedicated people armed with nothing but faith in Almighty God; their only weapon of defense was the *non-violence philosophy* that always worked in our favor. Our enemy did not really know how to deal with the non-violence approach. Case in point: One day when we marched down to the courthouse, Sheriff Jim Clark and his deputies were waiting for us. No sooner than we arrived, they had school buses lined up to take us to Camp Selma, which is a prison camp. This bus was full of freedom fighters, and as we were carted off to prison without a trial, we were singing and praying. A white man riding in the seat next to the driver had a double barrel shotgun in his hand. He shouted to us, "Shut up or I will shoot!" Of course we were afraid, but we never stopped singing and praying. Suddenly the man began crying like a little child. He did not know how to deal with non-violence. If we had been violent with him, he could have dealt with us with his shotgun, and they would have rewarded him for doing so.

The march on this day was greater than the one before. We had greater participation. In fact, the line stretched from Brown Chapel Church all the way to the courthouse. As I have said before, these were the "members of the ground crew." In a real sense they made the movement by showing up day after day and night after night. They were the company of the committed! Dr. King had said so many times, "If a man hasn't found something worth dying for he isn't fit to live." The people found worth in the right to register and vote.

They kept us in jail for several days and tried separating the leaders from the followers and telling the followers that the leaders had gotten out and had left them in jail, trying to discourage them. But it didn't work; the people took it as a joke, another one of the white man's tricks. They were willing to stay in jail until proper notice was given by the movement leaders.

Each night we would hold a mass meeting to teach workers the non-violence approach, to assess the various happenings of the day–what problems occurred today, did Jim Clark act up today, or did the federal judge rule against the march. Sure enough, at the height of the movement the judge put a halt to the march. We camped in the street in front of Brown Chapel for two weeks or more waiting for the order to be lifted. They thought the order would kill our spirits, and the movement would dry up. But we held a prayer vigil right at that spot in the street night and day. Even the rain and the cold never dampened our spirits or stopped the movement. I have never seen people so dedicated and committed before.

Somebody saw us standing in the rain and the cold and gave us a tent to shelter us. Instead of the stalling hurting the movement, it gave it a big boost. We had people in the church and under the tent. We called the tent the "Berlin wall." We would be under the tent and the cops and Sheriff's deputies would be camped about a stone's throw away, and they would harass us by shooting BB shots at us. One night they shot a young lady's front tooth out. People still continued to come and support the movement. Local people were there day and night.

To help in the struggle to get the right to vote, the leaders decided to boycott the downtown merchants in order to put pressure on the "powers that be," knowing every thing and every person has props and braces. The boycott would help to remove the props and braces from the Board of Registrars and other relative matters.

The boycott was very successful, especially the bus boycott. In fact, the bus company went out of business because of the effectiveness of the bus boycott in Selma, Alabama, in 1965. The boycott of the downtown merchants went well after the leaders of the movement "peeped their hold card."

Some of the stores encouraged their Negro customers to order what they wanted by phone and they would deliver the goods to them. We reminded these customers that we would be on watch for the delivery truck and/or car, et cetera. We also told the people that if they broke the picket line someone would take their picture and expose them by passing it out in the mass meetings. As a result of these tactics, we were able to have a successful merchant boycott. We encouraged the people to make do, or if need be, to go out of town to shop. As I recall, we had very good cooperation with a majority of the Negroes in Selma and Dallas County. Again, that's why I named them "the members of the ground crew." Had it not been for them we would not be where we are today. They had the power of stick-to-it-ness, that spirit that said don't quit until the job is done.

Of course the mood of the white community was: let them blow off steam. They'll "cool down in a few days." But those days turned into nights and those nights and days turned into weeks, and the weeks turned into months. The Negro had to learn the hard way that the oppressors never give up their privileges voluntarily. That must be demanded by the oppressed. Some wanted us to go slow, take it easy, don't rock the boat, follow customs and traditions, but we felt that waiting, customs, and traditions got us in the shape we were in! For centuries, everywhere we looked we saw racism and segregation. We saw "Colored only" water fountains, "White only" water fountains, and all the waters came from the same well. We saw "Colored only rest room," "White only rest room." What this really shows was that this was not a question of race, but one of color, because when it came to white only fountains, it doesn't matter what your race was, so long as your skin was white. We saw segregation in motels and hotels. When the signs in front of the hotels and motels said "No vacancy," it didn't mean they *really didn't have any vacancies, they just didn't have any for people of color.* We saw "Colored only" waiting rooms and "White only" waiting rooms in the bus stations. Dallas County has a public fishing lake, yet, this public lake was segregated. Black folks had to go to the back of this public lake to fish. Recently, former Mayor Joe Smitherman said, "Black folks have nine out of the top thirteen political positions in Selma, Alabama;" but what he ignored was that for years White folks had *all* of the best jobs—and the rest of the jobs too.

The City of Selma was a hard town to break down, racially speaking. It didn't want to give an inch; we tried to negotiate with the powers that be and for the longest time all we got was empty promises. Someone of good faith called a meeting of Whites and Blacks to sit down togther and establish some common ground. A few of us did meet, but when some Whites discovered that Blacks were going to be part of the meeting, I heard someone say, "I ain't never met with Negroes before and I'm not about to start now." That ended the meeting that day, and I was never called to another one of that kind.

We felt that we had to continue to demonstrate by holding mass meetings and marching back and forth down to the courthouse. We demonstrated to show the world how badly we were being treated by those in authority. We carried signs naming our complaints. The purposes of the mass meeting were to encourage, inform, instruct, and to teach people all they needed to know about the movement. We had some good mass meetings. We had people who could sing and were members of the choir. We had a Reverend Gallaway who played for the choir. Every freedom song somebody led, he could play—and there were many freedom songs.

You know, singing has its place. Some things you can't say, but you can sing it. The slave bosses didn't try to keep the slaves from singing, so when a secret meeting of slaves was announced, they had to find a way of informing each other without the straw bosses knowing about it. I remember whenever we had a strategy meeting, there was always an informer from the other side in our meeting getting information to take back. Like the slaves, we sang because singing was good for the soul—and it also served to inform the people. Someone would tell the trusted house boy, who also served as the water boy to those working in the field. The slaves gave the impression that they were happy, but they were not: They announced the meeting place by singing:

Steal away, steal away
Steal away, to Jesus
Steal away, steal away home,
I ain't got long to stay here

Somehow the slaves got the message secretly; they gathered together in the swamps late at night. They were concerned about whether or not they could be heard up in the big house, so they would use the same water boy to stand at the house and listen to see if he could hear anything from them. The boy, as he passed out water, began to sing:

Oh I couldn't hear nobody pray
Oh Lord, I couldn't hear nobody pray
I was way down yonder by myself,
But I couldn't hear nobody pray

This method was used to keep Mr. Charlie in the big house from hearing and knowing what was going on in the meeting. They all would have been punished had the plantation owner known of the meeting. It always worries white folks when

Negroes start meeting, especially when they meet to discuss their situation and the poor conditions under which they live. But unlike the slaves, the Negro didn't care who heard him or who knew about what he was doing. Instead of singing to one another, they sang to the oppressor loud and clear. They expressed their inward and outward feelings in song in the mass meetings and in the streets: "Ain't gonna let nobody turn me around . . ."

Our theme song was: "*We* shall overcome some day. . ."

It was the singing in the mass meetings that got everybody worked up and put us in a good mood for what was ahead. After the singing of freedom songs came preaching, and pep talks by various leaders of the movement. Plans for the next move were announced.

We still had to be carful not to say too much, because we never knew who was listening. We noticed one night an object standing near the pulpit, and when I inquired about it, we discovered that it was a listening device from one of the local radio stations. The mayor, probate judge, and a few more who I could not recognize were standing across the street from Brown Chapel listening to our every word. We got rid of that device and they could no longer listen in on us.

Then they sent a trooper or police officer to the meeting to check on what we were saying and/or doing. We would not knowingly allow them to stay in the meeting.

One trooper stopped Dr. King's car one night and wanted to know, "Why don't you allow my men to stay in the meeting?"

Upon which Dr. King replied, "Ask Reverend P.H. Lewis, the pastor of Brown Chapel."

The reason we had to screen our strategy sessions was that our enemies always knew what our next moves were. Then they would call and say they had been told that there was a bomb planted in the church, and they asked everyone to leave the building while they checked for the bomb. To my knowledge they never found a bomb. I really think that they thought that the threat of a bomb would scare people and they would stay away from the meeting place, but it had very little effect on keeping the people away. In fact, they hung on in there even when the going was tough. They said and they meant it, "We ain't gonna let nobody or nothing turn us around."

It has been alleged that the white citizen council invited Governor George Wallace to come to Selma and speak for them. This was some time in February,1965, when the movement was in its bloom. Dr. King was in the Selma jail. Governor Wallace came and spoke, and to the surprise of many, he said nothing about Dr. King being in jail or the movement. You know and I know there are some things you just can't ignore and they will go away. You can't ignore cancer—you must deal with it. The cancer of racism in this country must be dealt with. We cannot continue to ignore it by pretending that it doesn't exist and sweeping it under the rug while blacks folks and poor white folks suffer from it. They are abused by it daily.

George Wallace tried to talk about what kind of industries he was bringing into the state to fatten the pockets of the politician and greedy businessmen and said nothing about the suffering of the disinherited, dispossessed and the least of these that showed what he thought about Negroes and poor Whites.

The white citizen council also invited former Governor Ross Barnett, another segregationist, from Missiissippi to try to strengthen the cause of racism while the movement was going on in Selma, Alabama. When Governor Barnett came to Brown Chapel Church, we responded with kindness and courtesy. Governor Ross Barnett gained national attention when he tried and failed to keep Mr. James Meredeth from attending the University of Mississippi in 1962. Governor George Wallace stood in the schoolhouse door in 1963, trying to keep Miss Vivian Malone from entering in the University of Alabama, but he failed and she was able to enter and graduate.

We were not intimidated by Barnett and Wallace. In fact their coming to Selma encouraged us, because it gave ammunition to fire up the crowd in the mass meetings. Isn't it strange that white folks would accuse Negroes of bringing outside "agitators" into Selma when there were no bigger outside "agitators" than Governor George C. Wallace of Alabama and Governor Ross Barnett of Mississippi? Dr. King said in his "I have a dream" speech, "I have a dream that one day down in Alabama, with its vicious racists, with its governor's lips dripping with words of interposition and nullification . . ." He goes on to say, "I have a dream that even down in Mississippi, a state sweltering with the heat of injustice, sweltering with the heat of oppression, will be transformed into an oasis of freedom and justice."

It was speeches like this by Dr. Martin Luther King Jr, a great leader of the people, and not the speeches of the racists like Governors Wallace and Barnett that moved us. The record is clear: The Negro gained more freedom under Wallace and his kind than anyone else. They didn't intend it to be that way, but when the Negroes' backs were to the walls, they had no other choice but to come out swinging. So Governors Barnett and Wallace came to Selma, not to help the Negro cause, but the white folks, but instead it gave rise to the Negro movement. When you have people like Governor Wallace speaking publicly saying he stands for "segregation yesterday, segregation today, and segregation forever," especially when he holds the highest office in the state, it's time for every black person to become very concerned about their state of well-being. We were fired up and we decided that we were not going to take it any longer! We marched harder and longer, and we sang louder. We meant to be free!

We decided to push the issue a little further. Dr. King said let's announce that we are going to march at night. Now, with Wilson Baker public safety director, he said he could not guarantee us protection if we marched at night. He said that he only had about twenty-five officers and he didn't think that would be adequate enough if something happened at night. Mr. Baker also said that the word was out that if we marched at night, someone planned to kill Dr. King. The plan was to attack the marchers from the middle and from behind and draw attention from the front, thereby giving time to kill Dr. King.

The leaders thought it over and Dr. King decided not to march that night, but said perhaps another night.

Marchers enroute to Montgomery, on Highway 80 East. The man on crutches was one of 300 who marched the entire distance from Selma to Montgomery. Like many others, he was white.

Looking back on it, as I remember, it wasn't easy trying to convince him not to have a night march. He had what it took to be a leader—he was fearless and courageous. He was a born leader.

The final march from Selma to Montgomery was on March 21, 1965. Prayer was offered by Bishop Howard Primm, one of the African Methodist Episcopal church bishops. The march left the steps of Brown Chapel church led by Dr. Martin Luther King Jr, Ralph Abernathy, Ralph Bunche, F.D. Reese, and P.H. Lewis Sr, along with a vast host of supporters of the movement. We were walking in the right lane of Highway 80, going east to Montgomery, Alabama, our state capital. We marched so many miles on Sunday, March 21, and we rested, had a service, spent the night, left that campsite, walked so many miles on Monday, March 22, camped at that site, had a rally, and spent the night. Tuesday, March 23, the marchers left the camp site and walked some more miles to Montgomery; the marchers were now coming into the last stretch on March 24, which was Wednesday. Three-hundred-plus marched all the way, including a one-legged man who walked on crutches. When we left Brown Chapel on Sunday afternoon, the weather was perfect, but between Sunday and Wednesday it was typical March weather—plenty of rain, and in the swamps and the counties we had to pass through, there was plenty of mud. But the marchers endured it and finally ended up at St. Jude's building, where we spent the night and were entertained by movie stars.

Thursday morning we lined up and headed for the steps of the state capital, where many speakers were heard, and the climactic speech was made by Dr. King to a mammoth crowd of freedom-loving people, both black and white.

As a result of our efforts from January 2, 1965, to March 25, 1965 to gain the right to vote, we won the right to vote by the passing of the 1965 Voting Right Bill that did away with poll tax, literacy tests, and other devices that kept black folks from registering and voting.

A sheriff blocks a black man from voting in Selma, Alabama. The man in the center, with the sheriffs night stickin his abdomen, is Rev. P.H. Lewis.

II.

WHAT THE NEGROES IN SELMA AND DALLAS COUNTY WANT

Before expressing the present grievances of the Negroes in Selma, there are four questions that need to be answered, in order to clear up the misunderstanding that could hinder the effectiveness of our appeal and the implementation of steps toward alleviating the grievances.

1. WHY DID NEGROES DEMONSTRATE?

In September of 1963, we petitioned the city and county officials as well as the businessmen of Selma in an attempt to open the lines of communication that the grievances could be presented and discussed in a spirit of understanding and good will. Everyone at the time turned a deaf ear. We were forced to use other means to bring our grievances to the attention of the community and to those who refused to listen previously.

28

2. WHY DID OTHER CIVIL RIGHTS GROUPS "INVADE" OUR COMMUNITY?

They did not come without invitation. They were invited by the Dallas County Voter's League representing the Negro citizens. They constituted part of the other means spoken of in the answer to question number one. It was necessary to bring in sympathizers to do a job that, alone, our people could not do because of intimidation and reprisals.

Garrow/Selma
Document P/5

HENRY BROWNLEE
1/28/65

Distributed by:
Southern Christian Leadership Conference
Dr. Martin Luther King, Jr. President

3. WHY DID THE NEGROES NOT USE THE FIRST TEN-DAY PERIOD OFFER BY THE BOARD OF REGISTRARS BEFORE DR. KING CAME TO TOWN?

Negroes had learned from many regrettable experiences that our salvation rests in numbers. Many times before, polite doors have been opened only to be followed by intimidation and reprisal; literacy tests on interpretation of the constitution prove to be difficult.

4. IS THERE VOLUNTARY CO-OPERATION ON THE PART OF NEGROES IN GENERAL?

Yes! No one is forced to do anything. Some have hesitated to make full commitment due to fear of reprisals. Now determination has usurped fear. Everyone was committed to the drive for first class citizenship:

The Dallas County Voter's League, Business and Profession League, Selma Teacher's Association, Alpha Phi Alpha Fraternity, and the Chester Club. The question has been asked again and again by white folks, "What is it that black folks want and to what end will they go to achieve their just desire?" The answer is simple. Black folks want all the basic rights and privileges, as well as responsibilities of any other citizen of Selma and Dallas County.

THE FOLLOWING EIGHT GRIEVANCES WERE MOST PRESSING AT THE TIME:

1. Establishment of lines of communication between Whites and Blacks, chosen by their respective groups.

2. That every qualified person be permitted to register and vote without intimidation or reprisal.

3. All city and county officials, as well as business and professional leaders, take definite steps to have the registrar's office open at least forty hours per week, with consideration for those persons who are unable to make the four o'clock closing time; and that the numbering and vouching system be abolished.

4. Police brutality be discontinued immediately and that a definite policy against such acts be established, published, and enforced.

5. Fair employment practices be utilized in local and federal positions, county and city government, skilled and semi-skilled as well as unskilled labor and general public businesses.

6. All public facilities be opened to Negroes as stipulated in the Public Accommodation Section of the Civil Rights Act.

7. Representation in all city and county policy-making bodies, such as City Council, County Board of Revenue, Board of Education, et cetera.

8. That the white citizens recognize the dignity of the Negro and show the same by according him common courtesy such as title, (Mr., Miss, or Mrs.) et cetera, in all verbal and written communication and in the local newspaper.

It is hoped that the picture has been made clear that the Negro community is now concerned about these rights, and that we will not be satisfied until these rights are enjoyed by every citizen, whatever his race may be.

These eight grievances were never met by any of the city and county officials. We had no other choice but to hold mass meetings, and demonstrate in streets by marching down to the Dallas County courthouse by the hundreds and by the thousands. Finally we had to march to Montgomery after the "Bloody Sunday" incident, when people around the world saw on television and read the following day in the newspapers:

"Selma, Alabama, March 7, 1965, State Troopers and mounted deputies bombarded marching Negroes with tear gas today and then waded into them with clubs, whips, night sticks, cattle prods, and ropes. Hundreds of marchers were hurt. Among them was John Lewis, President of the Student Non-violent Coordinating Committee, who suffered a possible skull fracture."

III.

A VISITATION TO BE IGNORED

MARTIN LUTHER KING JR TO SELMA, ALABAMA, ON JANUARY 2, 1965; the headline in the Selma *Times Journal* read, "Visitation to be Ignored."

According to the news wire, a spokesman for M.L. King—the controversial darkie who FBI Director J. Edger Hoover recently branded as "the most notorious liar in the country" has announced that King would "speak at an Emancipation Proclamation" program in Selma and answer newsmen's questions afterward at a news conference." The article goes on to say that it was scarcely an event of significance, nor of any great consequence. "King has been here before and, no doubt, when he deems it expedient to visit Selma as a necessity to the process of maintaining the pious image he seeks to portray, he will return again.

"Obviously, since there was a degree of public attention focused on the civil rights proceedings conducted by three federal judges last week, and since that court is now recessed, the judiciary departed and racial agitation being comparatively quiet in other areas, this city apparently seemed the logical place for a Negro preacher to set up shop. This, of course, is simply a maneuver to provide a forum in which he can expound upon his current views at the expense of the sundry newsmen who will be attracted to the confab in anticipation of something sensational.

"So the man will come to town, speak, and hold a news conference and hope for a quantity of publicity. Well, this is his privilege and undoubtedly he will attempt to make the most of it. Frankly, we do not believe our responsible citizens, white or colored, will be much concerned with him one way or the other. After all, during past years we have survived several Ringling Brothers performances, a Jeanette McDonald concert, Al G. Fields and Lasses white minstrel shows, two world wars, a number of floods, the Democrats, Republicans and Colonel Bundy's rodeo."

To say "the responsible citizens, white or colored, would not be concerned with him one way or the other" proved to be untrue. I was pastor of Brown Chapel African Methodist Episcopal Church at that time, and I saw concern in the very first meeting we had on Saturday, January 2, 1965. The church seated around a thousand folks; that Saturday I saw standing room only, both White and Black, who came to hear Dr. Martin Luther King Jr., not only that Saturday, but every time Dr. King came to town. He could say it, and he always had something to say that was relevant. As my daddy used to say, "Don't ever call the cows unless you got something to give them." Dr. King always had something to give us, and we were hungry for it.

The article said that "this fellow isn't in the class with Ringling Brothers, Jeanette McDonald, two wars, floods," et

34

cetera, but I say, put them all together, they did not effect the City of Selma like that one solitary life, Dr. Martin Luther King Jr. He took the city, turned it inside out, upside down and left it right side up. The City of Selma, Dallas County, and the surrounding counties will never be the same again.

Dr. King was so successful in part because, ironically, the powers-that-be in Selma and Dallas County did not follow their own game plan to ignore the great leader's presence. To a great extent we were responsible for that. (See chapter VII.) Instead, when he and others led a march to the Selma Courthouse in February, 1965, authorities arrested all the leaders. The idea, apparently, was to cut off the snake's head so that the whole animal will die. The strategy backfired. From his jail cell Dr. King wrote the following letter, which was published in newspapers across the country:

A LETTER FROM DR. MARTIN LUTHER KING JR. FROM SELMA, ALABAMA JAIL

Dear Friend:

When the King of Norway participated in awarding the Nobel Peace Prize to me, he surely didn't think that in less than sixty days I would be in jail. He, and almost all world opinion will be shocked because they are little aware of the unfinished business in the South.

By jailing hundreds of Negroes, the city of Selma, Alabama, has revealed the persisting ugliness of segregation to the nation and the world. When the Civil Rights Act of 1964 was passed many decent Americans were lulled into complacency because they thought the day of difficult struggle was over.

Why are we in jail? Have you ever been required to answer one hundred questions on government, some obtuse even to a political science specialist, merely to vote? Have you ever stood in line with hundreds of others after waiting an entire day and seen less than ten given the qualifying test.

This is Selma, Alabama. There are more Negroes in jail with me than on the voting roles.

But apart from voting rights, merely to be a person in Selma is not easy. When reporters asked Sheriff Clark if a woman defendant was married, he replied, "She is a nigger woman and she hadn't got a Miss or a Mrs. in front of her name."

This is U.S.A. 1965. We are in jail simply because we cannot tolerate these conditions for our nation and for ourselves.

We need the help of decent Americans. Our organization, SCLC, is not only working in Selma, Alabama, but in dozens of others Southern communities. Our self-help projects operate in South Carolina, Georgia, Mississippi, Louisiana, and other Southern States. Our people are eager to work, to sacrifice, to be jailed, but their income, normally meager, is cut off in these crises. Your help can make the difference. Your help can be a message of unity, which the thickest jail walls cannot muffle. With warmest good wishes from all of us.

Sincerely,

Martin Luther King

Of course others continued to view the entire Black and rights movement as "a visitation to be ignored." One, with whom I strongly disagree is Attorney J.L. Chestnut, who, in his book *Black in Selma* stated that "all we got out of the movement was a B&P Supermarket." We won the right to vote in masses, we got rid of poll tax, the literacy test; we gained some human dignity, paved streets—you could always tell where the black community began because that's where the pavement ended. We got rid of Sheriff Jim Clark and his possemen, which symbolized the old southern denial to people of color, and we have been elected and hired in positions that we only dreamed of before 1965. Discrimination signs are down now. Even the rebel flag is off of the capital dome in the state of South Carolina.

I drove Dr. King to Wilcox county. Camden is the county seat. We went to two places: Camden Academy High School, where he spoke from the football diamond and received a warm reception, and then to the town of Camden. In Sheriff Lumme Jenking's town, where he has been the Sheriff for more than thirty-five years, he never carried a gun, but he had some fast feet. He was known for kicking, dogging, jailing, and killing Negroes. Dr. King had his rally on the jailhouse steps in Camden and he had a good crowd of black folks, and a lot of white folks peeped out of their office windows.

It was good that he went there. It made a difference. You see, before Dr. King went there in 1965, all elected officials were white, even though the ratio was eighty-five or ninety percent black.

Today there is a great change in elected public officials in Wilcox County. That's the way it ought to be: The majority should rule. However, Blacks should never treat white folks as Whites treated Negroes all of those years. It has been said, "A doctrine of black supremacy is worse than a doctrine of white supremacy."

IV.

THE JIM CROW LAW

The Jim Crow Law referred to the practices, institutions, and laws that support segregation of Negroes from whites. The term came into use in the 1880's and originally referred to a Negro character in an old song. In the 1820's it was the name of a popular dance. Jim Crow laws in certain southern states required separation of the races in such places as public conveyances, restaurants, hotels, schools, factories and theaters.

These six places of separation were drawn up by some white men to keep the white and colored races apart, but some white men broke their own laws by having relationships with black women. It is an undeniable fact. All one has to do is look in the race; it's so spotted it's a shame to read the so-called "Jim Crow Law" and what it represented.

I was in Chicago, Illinois, in 1965 speaking at a civil rights rally, and a newsman asked me what I thought about integration. Before I could answer him, a white lady ran up and said, "Let me answer that question! The white man and the black woman integrated in the moonlight, but the black man and the white woman will integrate in the sunlight."

It's very strange how white folks put on public fronts about integration, but in the dark we are all the same color. The black woman cooks his food, cleans his floors, raises his children. Yet, when she is taken home by the white man she has to sit in the back seat. Why?

Another question comes to mind: Why were some white men fighting so hard against integration in the school? It was not that he didn't want black children to go to school with his children in public school. We have been doing that a long time. He doesn't want you to go to school with his wife's children. It seems the "Jim Crow Laws" were designed to keep black folks in their places, but the white man, the maker of the laws, has had an open season on black women. It reminds me of a passage in the Bible, found in St. Matthew the 23rd chapter and beginning at the thirteenth verse:

13. "But woe unto you scribes and Pharisees, hypocrites! For you shut up the kingdom of heaven against men: for ye neither go in yourselves, neither suffer ye them that are entering to go in.
14. Woe unto you, scribes and Pharisees, hypocrites! For you devour widows' houses and for a pretense make long prayer: therefore ye shall receive the greater damnation.
15. Woe unto you scribes and Pharisees, hypocrites! For ye compass sea and the land to make one proselyte, and when he is made, ye make him twofold more the child of hell than yourselves.
16. Woe unto you, ye blind guides which say, Whosoever shall swear by the temple, it is nothing; but whosoever shall swear by the gold of the temple, he is a debtor!
17. Ye fools and blind: For whether is greater, the gold, or the temple that sanctifieth the gold?

18. And, Whosoever shall swear by the altar, it is nothing; but whosoever sweareth by the gift that is upon it, he is guilty.

19. Ye fools and blind: For whether is greater, the gift, or the altar that santifieth the gift?

20. Whoso therefore shall swear by the altar, sweareth by it, and by all things thereon.

21. And whoso shall swear by the temple, sweareth by it, and by him that dwelleth therein.

22. And he that shall swear by heaven, sweareth by the throne of God, and by him that sitteth thereon.

23. Woe unto you, scribes and Pharisees, hypocrites! For ye pay tithe of mint and anise and cummin, and have omitted the weightier matters of the law, judgment, mercy, and faith: these ought ye to have done, and not to leave the other undone.

24. Ye blind guides, which strain at a gnat, and swallow a camel.

25. Woe unto you scribes and Pharisees, hypocrites! For ye make clean the outside of the cup and clean the platter, but within they are full of extortion and excess."

V.

THE HISTORY OF NEGRO POLITICAL PARTICIPATION

Since the franchise was first guaranteed to Negroes, there has been a history of efforts in the south to render the guaranteed meaningless. As devices have been struck down, others have been adopted in their place. The end of the Civil War did not immediately bring the right of suffrage to the ex-slaves. The former confederate states still were governed by the same men who had led during seccession. The legal rights that Negroes had were little better than they had under slavery.

The reconstruction program of 1867 took power away from the white southern governments and gave it to the military rulers of the five military districts established under the radical reconstruction legislature. These military rulers, within a year, registered more than 700,000 Negroes to vote, slightly more than the number of Whites then registered in the south. The Freedmen's Bureau tried to inform the Negroes of their new political rights and to protect them in the exercise of those rights. Dissatisfied with those temporary suffrage arrangements in the reconstruction legislation, and with provisions in the Fourteenth Amendment unclear regarding franchise, the Congress proposed the Fifteenth Amendment, which became a part of the Constitution on March 30, 1870.

This amendment contains the declaration that the right to vote shall not be denied on account of race, color, or previous condition of servitude. The Fourteenth and especially the Fifteenth Amendment were the law of the land ever since March of 1870, and those persons who were elected to office, such as the President, the Congressmen, State Representatives, Governors, Senators, State Attornies General, Mayors, Councilmen, et cetera, all swore with hand on the Bible to uphold the laws of the Constitution of The United States.

It is my understanding that the United States Constitution takes precedent over any state, city or county laws. In too many instances, laws were violated and downright ignored by publicly elected officials, and that caused a lot of heartaches for black folks in America. It is shocking to discover how cruelly black folks have been treated, and all we had to go through, just to get the right to vote and other rights guaranteed to us because we are citizens of the United States.

I agree with James Weldon Johnson, writer of the Negro Spiritual, "*Lift Every Voice and Sing*," especially in the second stanza: "Stony the road we trod, bitter the chastening rod, felt in the days when hopes unborn have died; yet with a steady beat, have not our weary feet come to the place for which our fathers sighed. We have come over a way that with tears has been watered. We have come treading our path through the blood of the slaughtered; Out from the gloomy past, till now we stand at last where the white gleam of our bright star is cast." The words of this hymn speak of the Negro's plight in the 1870's as well as in 2001. We have come a long way, but still have a long way to go, before achieving full equality.

The 1890 Mississippi Constitutional Convention adopted the scheme of requiring as a prerequisite for voting registration "reasonable" interpretation of the Constitution that would eliminate the Negro vote without obviously violating the Fifteenth Amendment. Between 1895 and 1910 other southern states set up similar qualifications, including Alabama, and especially the city of Selma and the county of Dallas. Then they added additional requirements such as the "good character" tests, enacted disfranchising constitutions which required the payment of a poll tax, set up property tax, and required applicants to pass literacy tests and a civic understanding test. Throughout the south, residency requirements were lengthened and the list of disfranchising crimes expanded to include offenses believed more often committed by Negroes, such as petty larceny. To assure white control even in predominantly negro localities, electoral machinery was centralized, and in most of the states registration and election officials were given broad discretion, and were appointed as state, rather than local, officials.

But even if the Negroes did learn to read, and acquire sufficient property, and remember to pay the poll tax and to keep the receipt on file, they could even then be tripped by the final bridle devised for them, the "white primary." This was a declaration by the Democratic Party that only whites were eligible for membership or allowed a voice in the nomination of party candidates. Since nomination by the Democratic Party in the south amounted to winning election, disbarment from the nominating process was the equivalent of disfranchisement.

The earliest primaries had been local, informal, and unregulated by law. Statutory recognition and regulation began in the mid-1880's and soon spread throughout the south. Permission was given to the parties either to formulate rules of membership themselves or to impose qualifications beyond those laid down by

43

statute. By 1930, in eleven southern states, the Democratic Party barred the Negro from a share in the nominating process by statewide rules, by rules of the county, or the city of the Democratic committee that restricted Negroes to nonpartisan and special elections and to general elections in which their Republican votes were a mere gesture.

Because of such devices, and the Negro's growing psychological and economic dependence upon the white man, intimidation by violence became less and less necessary to assure that the Negro would stay away from the polls and cease to run for office. However, Whites did use such tactics as massing at the polls to keep Republicans and Independents from voting, stuffing of ballot boxes, use of boxes with false bottoms, manipulation of the vote counts, and tampering with the registration books. Polling places were set at points removed from the Negro communities, and the location of polling places was changed without notice. Sometimes Negroes were told of a change which never was made.

It is one thing to read about the history of all the schemes set by white folks to keep Blacks away from the polls, but it is another thing to have lived through it. I remember back in 1958 in Wilcox county, Alabama, I had been to a meeting at the Tuskegee Institute, as it was called at that time. The late Dr. Edward talked about the right to vote and its importance. He asked how many people present were registered voters. Very few hands went up; my hand did not go up. Neither did a majority of those in the class. Edward asked how many had tried to register. Very few hands went up. He asked all of us to go back to our home county and try to get registered.

As soon as I got back home in Wilcox county, I asked someone to tell me where you go to get registered to vote. I went where they told me, and when I explained what I was there for, one lady said to the other lady, "Hey, do you know what he's talking about? I don't have the slightest idea." The other person said, "Tell him to go and ask the sheriff. I'm sure he can tell him where it is."

With good common sense, I didn't go to see the sheriff, but instead I went to see a Reverend Willie Frank Rubens, who ran an upholstery shop on one of the main streets in Camden. In fact, I was one of his employees. I decided to ask Reverend Rubens what he thought about registering and voting?

Boy, did he go off on me! "You can't do that in this county! You are no Martin Luther King!"

I went to work that day as usual, but the next morning, when I hit the door, he walked up to me and said, "Reverend, my wife and I have decided that we can't use you anymore." Of course I wanted to know why. He said, "I'm not going to lose my business here fooling with you trying to vote." I never worked for him another hour after that, but three years later, he lost that business, his home, and all his possessions, and it wasn't because he was trying to vote. In fact he had to leave town.

I had an opportunity to talk with him on several occasions after he lost his business. He said, "All I could see at that time was that good old dough rolling in." He asked me to forgive him, for what he did. After 1965, he became a registered voter in Montgomery, Alabama. He is now deceased. He had seven or eight children; I would love to hear from some of them. His children and I went to Camden Academy High School together.

So, the right to register and vote has not been so easy, because there have been forces without and forces within. But I'm like the farmer in Iowa getting his potatoes ready for the market. The first farmer took the time and put the small potatoes on the bottom and the big ones on the top; the other farmer was in a rush, so he just loaded his in the wagon, big ones and little ones together. Someone asked him why he didn't separate them.

He said, "There is no need to separate them, because over rough roads, the big ones always rise to the top."

Yes, Negroes have had some rough roads to travel, but like the moral of the story, "The big ones always rise to the top." In spite of all the scheming, diluting of votes, slate voting, good character tests, literacy tests, violence, intimidation, reapportionment, voters' identifications, et cetera, we are still a long way from the bottom. It was John Welder Johnson who said, "It is not the height that we have obtained, but the depth from whence we have come."

A multiplicity of questions arise in my mind when I read where white folks worked so hard and long to keep the Negro away from the polls and away from the political processes. They seem to be obsessed with hot passion to keep Blacks out of office, and will elect themselves as if the office automatically belonged to them. It is alleged that a certain candidate was running for the office of the Presidency; he spent something like twenty-nine million dollars of his own money running for a job that paid less than two hundred thousand dollars a year. You wonder why. It has to be more than meets the eye. It would be nice if we in America could live as Christian sisters and brothers; instead we are living and acting like cats and dogs. We must learn to live together as brothers and sisters or we will die like fools. There's enough on Planet Earth for everyone. The pie is big enough for all of us to get a slice, and everyone will be happy.

VI

THE GRANDFATHER CLAUSE

The grandfather clause describes measures added to seven State Constitutions between 1895 and 1910 in order to allow white men to vote while depriving Negroes of the privilege. The Constitutions set up such a high requirement for voting that they even deprived many white men of their votes. The States then granted exemptions to anyone who had the right to vote on January 1, 1867, and to his lineal descendants, and because no Negro had voted in the south before 1867, and because the voting requirements were especially high, these clauses disfranchised almost all Negroes.

In 1915, the Supreme Court of the United States declared the grandfather clause unconstitutional. But for almost half a century, this nonsensical grandfather clause deprived Negroes of their right to register and vote, before someone did something about it. We already got the idea.

This of course is another one of the many unjust laws that good men in office allowed in their cities, counties, and their states. So many times I hear elected officials using the phrases "law and order," "upholding the laws." Is it morally right for any elected public official to enforce unjust laws that attack rights guaranteed by the Constitution of the United States? Many of the southern states did, and tried to get away with it, but when a case was tested in high court, it was declared unconstitutional.

It is always disturbing when I hear white folks asking, "What is it that black folks want?" We want everything every other blue and red blooded American wants on the bases of equality and equal opportunity. If you are a student of history you should know that we want all that belongs to the Negro as granted by law. You must look on "the other side of 1965" to really see why the Negroes were demonstrating, holding mass meetings and walking from Selma to Montgomery. We had reached the point in history where we were determined to free ourselves at any cost. This does not apply only to the more aggressive or even better educated or more affluent Blacks, but rather to the entire black race, embracing all classes and conditions. Blacks have gotten to the place where we were fired-up and fed-up, and couldn't take any more.

That's why it is important to see "the other side of Selma, 1965." Bear in mind that change, even of an idea, does not happen at a particular point and time. It builds in history. Any great change must be traced to its beginning, not to the moment of a particular crisis, but must go back in history to find the source, the originator of the idea, the person or persons who formulated the concept in order to understand what was happening in 1965. Just to see the fire and not trace it's beginning is unwise, to say the least.

It was indeed paradoxical that Americans themselves were seeking freedom from British oppression and at the same time holding Negroes in bondage for life.

VII.

WHY I OPENED THE DOORS OF BROWN CHAPEL A.M.E. CHURCH IN 1965

Following the Civil War, the "Black Codes" gave Blacks equal rights in the United States, but no laws prohibited segregation. In fact, in 1890, the state of Louisiana passed a statute ordering "that all railway companies carrying passengers in their coaches in this state shall provide equal but separate accommodations for the white and colored races, by providing two or more passenger coaches for each passenger train, or by dividing the passenger coaches by a partition so as to secure separate accommodations. . . ." Violators were either fined $25 or sentenced to twenty days in jail.

Homer Plessy, a thirty-year-old shoemaker, seven-eighths white and one-eighth black, was jailed for sitting in the Whites Only Car of the East Louisiana Railroad.

Plessy pleaded in court that the Separate Car Act violated the Thirteenth and Fourteenth Amendments of the Constitution. Judge John Howard Ferguson ruled that, since the railroad had no operations outside the state of Louisiana, state law applied and Plessy was guilty of refusing to leave the white car.

Plessy appealed to the Supreme Court of Louisiana, and lost again. He appealed to the United States Supreme Court and in 1896, that august body found Homer Plessy guilty once more. The prosecutor's case is printed below. The one dissenter to the verdict was Justice John Harlan. He wrote, "Our Constitution is color-blind, and neither knows nor tolerates classes among citizens. In respect to civil rights, all persons are equal before the law . . . In my opinion the judgment this day rendered will, in time, prove to be quite as pernicious as the decision made by this tribunal in the Dred Scott case . . . The present decision, it may well be apprehended, will not only stimulate aggressions, more or less brutal and irritating, upon the admitted rights of colored citizens, but will encourage the belief that it is possible, by means of state enactments, to [render impotent] the recent amendments to the Constitution."

Yet, it wasn't until the 1954 decision in Brown v. Board of Education, discussed in another chapter, that the "separate but equal" concept would finally be defeated.

On July 5, 1964, President Johnson signed the 1964 Civil Rights Bill. The same night in Selma, Alabama, there was a race riot. It has been alleged that it was staged to prove a point. The climate in Selma was very tense. A few days later, Judge James Hare, with the support of Governor George Wallace, issued his infamous injunction prohibiting mass meetings to discuss the Civil Rights Bill, stating that no more than three people could meet. Judge Hare ordered the Dallas County sheriff's department to serve official injunction papers to the following organizations and persons: the Ku Klux Klan, the National States Rights Party, every civil rights organization he could think of, and the following pastors of black churches: Reverend I.C. Acoff of Morning Star

Baptist Church, Earnest Bradford of Northern Height Presbyterian Church, Claude Brown of Knox Presbyterian Church, M.C. Cleveland of First Baptist Church, M.S. Hasty of Ward Chapel A.M.E. Church, C.C. Hunter of Hunter Chapel A.M.E. Church, William Kemp of Providence Baptist Church, P.H. Lewis of Brown Chapel A.M.E. Church, Charles A. Lett of Green Street Baptist Church, F.D. Reese of Ebenezer Baptist Church, Henry Plunkett of Antioch A.M.E. Church, L.L. Anderson of Tabernacle Baptist Church, and W.T. Minetee, the Presiding Elder of the Selma District A.M.E. Church. The punishment for violation of this injunction was a stiff fine and incarceration. We of the Dallas County Voter's League felt that our backs were to the wall.

The Voter's League asked several pastors to allow meetings to be held in their church, and all refused. I, too, was asked and said no. The second time I was asked, I said yes.

I decided to open the doors of Brown Chapel A.M.E. Church when I realized that this was not the first time I had been under an injunction and probation. When I was born, the mere fact that my face was black put me on probation and under an injunction. I could not attend the best schools in the county where I lived or even buy a small bottle of Coca Cola (it was made for white folks), nor could we black folks be seen on the streets in Camden, Alabama, after dark. The city would blow a whistle, which meant it was time for all black folks to leave the streets immediately. We were forbidden from riding in the front of the bus, and were made to ride in the front of the train because the front was the noisiest. When we black folks purchased Prince Albert loose cigarette tobacco, we were required to say *Mr.* Prince Albert tobacco. I have given all these examples to illustrate some of the forms of probation and injunctions that we as black people suffered and endured.

51

Another reason that I, as pastor of Brown Chapel A.M.E. Church, opened the doors to the civil rights movement, is that I am a "Son of Richard Allen," founder of the African Methodist Episcopal (A.M.E.) Church. The A.M.E. church was founded in 1787 in a blacksmith shop in Philadelphia, Pennsylvania.

Finally, I opened the doors of Brown Chapel A.M.E. Church, because I was never served the official injunction papers from Judge Hare. When the deputy sheriff rang my doorbell, and I answered the door, the deputy asked, "Does T.H. Lewis live here?" I answered, "No!" He turned and walked away. My name is P.H. Lewis, not T.H. Lewis. I knew that this technicality would not stand up in court, but it helped me make up my mind about opening the doors of Brown Chapel A.M.E. Church.

The threat of jail time that the injunction carried was an empty scare tactic. Black folks were being jailed for nothing anyway, so I thought, "Let them put us in jail for something!" The doors of Brown Chapel A.M.E. Church were opened because black folks were "sick and tired of being sick and tired!" Sick of being beaten, threatened, and cursed by the policemen and the sheriff. Tired of working all day in the kitchens, shops, and fields of white folks, doing the hardest and dirtiest work, sick of not being paid enough to feed, clothe, and house our children and ourselves. Sick of poor schools that led to poor jobs, sick of smelly outhouses and tired of unpaved streets that became mud holes when it rained. Tired of being ruled by racist public officials, sick of being labeled half-human and unable to govern ourselves; sick and tired of being embarrassed, brutalized, and insulted when all we wanted to do was exercise our right to register and vote.

Prior to 1965, fewer than one percent of black folks were registered to vote in Dallas county, out of an eligible thirteen thousand . However, there were 64 percent white registered voters out of an eligible twelve thousand.

The Dallas County Voter's League, led by F.D. Reese (president) and myself (vice-president), invited Dr. Martin Luther King to be the speaker at our Emancipation program, January 2, 1965. Dr. King accepted the invitation. The meeting place was Brown Chapel A.M.E. Church. Public announcements went out, people came, both black and white. Dr. King was late arriving, but the crowd waited to hear him.

When Dr. King spoke, his words seemed to have ridden the wind of the evening and everyone was caught up in his speech. We were moved from apathy and complacency to motivation and action. We were encouraged to become first-class citizens by registering to vote. Dr. King promised that we would become registered voters in masses, and he promised to come back again and again until we had the right to vote.

The Dallas County Voter's League had meetings every week, and as the movement progressed and grew, we met every day and night. We organized and held marches to the courthouse to register voters on a daily basis. At night we would have mass meetings to give thanks and praise to God, access our strategy, and teach people the non-violent approach.

An important part of the mass meetings was the freedom songs. In a sense the freedom songs are the soul of the movement. They are more than just incantations of clever phrases designed to invigorate a campaign; they are as old as the history of the Negro in America. They are adaptations of the songs the slaves sang—the sorrow songs, the shouts for joy, the battle hymns and the anthems of our movement. I have heard people talk of their beat and rhythm, but we in the movement are as inspired by their words. "Woke up this morning with mind stayed on freedom" is a sentence that needs no music to make its point. We sing the freedom songs today for the same reason the slaves sang them, because we, too, are in bondage and the songs add hope to our determination that, "We shall overcome, Black and White together. We shall overcome some day." I have stood in a meeting with hundreds of youngsters and joined in while they sang, "Ain't Gonna Let Nobody Turn Me 'Round." It is not just a song; it is a resolve. A few minutes later, I have seen those same youngsters refuse to turn around from the onrush of Possemen, refuse to turn around before a pugnacious Sheriff Jim Clark in command of men armed with power hoses. These songs bind us together, give us courage together, help us to march together.

Toward the end of the mass meeting, Hosea Williams or James Beverly would extend an appeal for volunteers to serve in our nonviolent army. We made it clear that we would not send anyone out to demonstrate who had not convinced himself and us that he could accept and endure violence without retaliating. At the same time, we urged the volunteers to give up any possible weapons that they might have on their persons.

Hundreds of people responded to this appeal. Some of those who carried penknives, Boy Scout knives—all kinds of knives—wanted to use them against the police and other attackers, especially against Jim Clark's possemen. We proved to them that we needed no weapons—not so much as a toothpick. We proved that we possessed the most formidable weapon of all—the conviction that we were right. We had the protection of our knowledge that we were more concerned about realizing our righteous aims than about saving our skins.

The invitational periods at the mass meetings, when we asked for volunteers, were much like those invitational periods that occur every Sunday morning in Negro churches, when the pastor projects the call to those present to join the church. By the twenties and thirties and forties, people came forward to join our army. (We did not hesitate to call our movement an army. But it was a special army, with no supplies but its sincerity, no uniform but its conscience. It was an army that would move but not maul. It was an army that would sing but not slay. It was an army that would flank but not falter. It was an army to storm bastions of hatred, to lay siege to the fortresses of segregation, to surround symbols of discrimination. It was an army whose allegiance was to God and whose strategy and intelligence were the eloquently simple dictates of conscience.)

As the meetings continued and as the battle for the soul of Selma quickened and caught the attention of the world, the meetings were more crowded and the volunteers more numerous. Men, women, and children came forward to shake hands, and then proceeded to the back of the church, where the Leadership Training Committee made an appointment with them to come to our office the following day for screening and intensive training. The focus of these training sessions were the socio-dramas designed to prepare the demonstrators for some of the challenges they could expect to face. The harsh language and physical abuse of the police and the self-appointed guardians of the law were frankly presented, along with the nonviolent creed in action: to resist without bitterness; to be cursed and not reply; to be beaten and not hit back. The S.C.L.C. staff who conducted these sessions played their roles with the conviction born of experience. They included the Reverend James Lawson, expelled from Vanderbilt University a few years earlier for his militant civil rights work, and one of the country's leading exponents of the nonviolent credo; the Reverend James Bevel, already and experienced leader in Nashville, Greenwood, and other campaigns; his wife Diane Nash Bevel, who as a student at Fisk had become an early symbol of the Negro's thrust toward freedom; the Reverend Bernard Lee, whose devotion to civil rights dated back to his leadership of the student movement at Alabama State College; the Reverend Andy Young, our able and dedicated program director; and Dorothy Cotton, director of our ongoing Citizenship Education Program, who also brought her talent for song to the heart of the movement.

Not all who volunteered could pass our strict tests for service as demonstrators. But there was much to be done, over and above the dramatic act of presenting one's body in the marches. There were errands to be run, phone calls to be made, clerical work such as typing, so many things. If a volunteer wasn't suited to march, he was utilized in one of a dozen other ways to help the cause. Every volunteer was required to sign a Commitment Card that read:

I hereby pledge myself—my person and body—to the non-violent movement. Therefore I will keep the following ten commandments:

1. MEDITATE daily on the teachings and life of Jesus.
2. REMEMBER always that the nonviolent movement in Selma seeks justice and reconciliation—not victory.
3. WALK and TALK in the manner of love, for God is love.
4. PRAY daily to be used by God in order that all men might be free.
5. SACRIFICE personal wishes in order that all men might be free.
6. OBSERVE with both friends and foe the ordinary rules of courtesy.
7. SEEK to perform regular service for others and for the world.
8. REFRAIN from the violence of fist, tongue, or heart.

9. STRIVE to be in good spiritual and bodily health.
10. FOLLOW the directions of the movement and of the captain on a demonstration.

I sign this pledge, having seriously considered what I do and with the determination and will to persevere.

Name_____

Address_____

Phone_____

Nearest Relative_____

Address_____

Besides demonstrations, I could also help the movement by: (Circle the proper items)

Run errands, drive my car, fix food for volunteers, clerical work, make phone calls, answer phones, mimeograph, type, print signs, distribute leaflets.

Dr. King and others including James Bevel, Andy Young. Hosea Williams, and C.T. Vivan, taught us the nonviolent approach. At last we were ready to face Sheriff Jim Clarke (Dallas County Sheriff) and his posse, with nothing but our faith in God and our bodies.

We had peaceful marches from Brown Chapel A.M.E. Church to the courthouse. Sheriff Clarke wanted us to come to the back door through the alley, but we went to the front entrance down the street. On several occasions we were met by Dallas County deputies and given three minutes to disburse or be jailed. We were prepared to go to jail and we did. (See chapter III.) We did not move as Sheriff Clarke announced that we were all under arrest. They loaded us on school buses and hauled us off to jail. They booked us like we were common criminals. We were fingerprinted and had our mugshots taken.

It was our strategy to be arrested and remain in jail. By using this strategy we would "break" the county. The county would have to feed us, hire extra personnel, and spend more on utilities.

On one occasion, sixty-five of us were locked in one big room, "The Bull Room," with one toilet, thirty-five cots, and blankets. We were given one big bucket of water with a dipper and fed three meals a day, consisting of peas and bread for breakfast, bread and peas for lunch and peas and bread for dinner. There were young and old in this group, but this time it was mostly elderly people. I remember sitting with my chin resting in my hand, and an eighty-five-year-old man said to me, "Cheer up, Reverend, everything is gonna be all right." Even though this eighty-five-year-old man had endured segregation and oppression his entire life, he still had the faith and the strength to encourage others and fight for freedom and equality.

During this same period of incarceration the temperature dropped to 16 degrees. There were only thirty-five blankets but sixty-five people, and the heat was turned off in "The Bull Room." It was so cold that night, but somehow we made it through and we awoke singing, "I woke up this morning and my mind stayed on freedom. Hallelujah! Hallelujah! I ain't gonna let nobody turn me around, ain't gonna let George Wallace turn me around, ain't gonna let Jim Clark and his posse turn me around!"

Within the next day or so I was taken from the Selma jail to Heflin, Alabama, (about 150 miles away). I was put in eighteen different state trooper cars and had a total of thirty-six trooper escorts. Once in Heflin, I was jailed by the Justice of the Peace. Again I was treated like a common criminal, but this time it was over a traffic ticket. The jail was in the home of the Justice of the Peace and I stayed there for three days, until my trial. I was fined $72.00 and returned to the Selma jail. On the return trip I was again transported in eighteen different state trooper cars and escorted by thirty-six different state troopers. There was one trooper who was kind to me, and the others were prejudiced and what we called "redneck."

Once I was back in Selma, the officers of Brown Chapel A.M.E. Church secured my release so that I could resume my pastoral duties as well as the organization of the mass meetings. Again we met day and night. It was a continuous thing.

Dr. Martin Luther King Jr., right, confronts a registrar in a Selma, Alabama, courthouse during an effort to register Blacks to vote. March, 1965.

It seemed as though we were not making much progress with the daily marches to the courthouse, and we were becoming restless and discouraged. James Bevel (one of Dr. King's lieutenants) was at his wit's end and full of frustration during a meeting in my home. He didn't know what we needed to do next, but he had an idea he wanted to discuss. He suggested that

59

we march from Selma to Montgomery, appeal to a higher source, and get more media coverage. At that time we were receiving media coverage only from the Selma *Times Journal*. We needed more media coverage and exposure to get to the world outside of Selma. We felt that the walk from Selma to Montgomery would break the stalemate and help us gain our voting rights.

At our next meeting, we discussed this idea with the other leaders and decided to prepare for the march from Selma to Montgomery. The date was set for March 7, 1965, the first Sunday in March. It would begin from the steps of Brown Chapel A.M.E. Church. We secured a permit, but the permit allowed only three hundred people to march.

On March 7, 1965, we lined up double file and began the march from Selma to Montgomery. Everything went along as expected until the marchers reached the Edmund Pettus Bridge. At the foot of the bridge, the marchers were met by a blockade of state troopers and possemen, with cattle prods, night sticks, tear gas, and enough hatred in their hearts to use all of the weapons they had. A man with a bullhorn called out, "Halt your march, turn around and go back to your church! You got two minutes."

We stood still.

Suddenly, about two dozen state troopers, swinging their clubs, rushed ahead of the column. Pushing and clubbing, they drove the Negroes back about fifty yards and then began firing tear gas. The gas bombs boomed like gunshots and a dense cloud like yellow smoke enveloped the screaming, helpless and defenseless Negroes. The Troopers charged into the gas-dazed Negroes again, and from behind the column, Sheriff Jim Clark's horse-mounted possemen charged in, swinging clubs and using cattle-prods. The hysterical Negroes broke and ran back to Brown Chapel African Methodist Episcopal Church where the march originated. Those who fled in other directions, between buildings, were quickly headed off by the hard-riding possemen. As the Negroes screamed through the town toward the church, where they had started their march, the possemen darted in after them, clubbing them down. Several witnesses said they saw horsemen use bullwhips and lengths of ropes to flog the fleeing Negroes.

The marchers in the front were beaten the worst. All of us ran back to the church as fast as we could. No sooner had we entered the sanctuary and parsonage than Sheriff Clarke and his possemen arrived. They lined up single file in front of the church and parsonage as if they were going to storm the buildings and massacre us. We were afraid for our lives.

Sheriff Jim Clark and his deputies. Others, called the possemen, were on horseback.

At that moment, Wilson Baker, the Selma City Public Safety Director, drove up. Safety Director Baker told Sheriff Clark, "You are on my turf now. Leave the marchers alone." Sheriff Clarke and his possemen left. Thank God for the attitude of Wilson Baker.

Meanwhile, inside the parsonage a group of doctors and nurses were gathered to treat the injured marchers. My wife's dining table became a makeshift hospital table. The doctors and nurses treated marchers for tear gas exposure, bruises, cuts, and other abrasions.

Then the soul-searching and healing began. We were both mentally and physically wounded. We called Dr. King, who was in Atlanta at the time, to tell him of the latest events. He asked if anyone was hurt and wanted all those that were injured

After the violence on March 7, 1965, the parsonage of Brown Chapel was converted into a makeshift hospital. The Reverend P.H. Lewis stands in the doorway, right. Courtesy of the National Voting Rights Museum, Selma, Alabama.

to go to the hospital. Those who required additional medical attention were taken to the Good Samaritan Hospital. Dr. King sent out an SOS throughout the nation asking clergymen to come to Selma.

During the march, national and international television and newspaper journalist were hidden in the bushes at the foot of the Edmund Pettus Bridge. These journalist documented the blatant brutality the marchers experienced and labeled March 7, 1965, "Bloody Sunday." The pictures and the film coverage were sent and seen around the world. When people saw the pictures of the brutality on the Edmund Pettus Bridge and man's inhumanity to man, they were shocked and horrified.

One anonymous writer sent the following letter to a local paper:

Record of Shame in Alabama That Will Be Hard to Erase

Alabama lawmen, given their head by Governor George Wallace, are writing a record of shame that they and their state will be a long time living down. What atonement is there for clubbing men, women, and children for asserting their right to walk on the public highways of Alabama? How sickening it is to hear Governor Wallace and his sympathizers carry on about "the southern way of life!"

They have shown the world what they really stand for, and it is uncomfortably reminiscent of what S.S. stood for in the early 1930's in Germany. Exaggeration, you say? Well, both share a belief in the myth of racial superiority. The Nazis and the racists of Alabama both turned to brutality and terror as a political weapon.

They share a common disdain for democratic principles. The Nazis justified their actions by appeals to emotion, to hate, by manufacturing scapegoats, and by raising the specter of Communism.

The Alabama racists blame everything on "outsiders," while beating Negroes who have lived in Selma or Marion or elsewhere in the black belt all their lives. They also call all who disagree with them communists or traitors. This is what they called other Alabamians, Whites in this case, who also marched to protest the treatment accorded Negro citizens. The fact that these Whites took the risks and the slurs is heartening evidence that there exists a reservoir of aroused decency in the white community in the deep south. These are the people who will have to pick up the pieces the madmen leave behind. Let it be empathized once more that the conflict in Alabama is over the right for Negro citizens to register to vote. This right is guaranteed them by the Constitution of the United States.

—Anonymous

Almost immediately, people began to converge on Selma. The first group to come were forty Roman Catholic seminary students from Los Angeles, California, and then came people from everywhere. We received all kinds of donations, clothes, portable toilets, money, food, letters, et cetera.

In my opinion, if Governor George Wallace, Sheriff Jim Clarke, the state troopers, and the possemen had left us alone, we would never have been able to complete the march from Selma to Montgomery. We were not prepared and did not have the necessary supplies and protection to go the distance. We owed the success of that march in part to our enemies.

64

On March 9, 1965, President Lyndon B. Johnson held a press conference to address "Bloody Sunday." It was televised and broadcast nationwide. President Johnson declared that the marchers in Selma would have federal protection along the entire route from Selma to Montgomery. In addition, he would ask Congress to pass a voting rights bill that would require mass registration and do away with the devices of the past that kept people from becoming registered voters.

President Johnson federalized a large number of National Guard units to protect the church, parsonage, and marchers. A federal trooper was placed at every door and window of the parsonage. (I have to acknowledge the loyalty of the federal troops, because many of them wore confederate flags on their helmets, but gave 100 percent to their commander-in-chief, President Johnson.) The President closed his address by quoting our theme song, "We shall overcome, deep in my heart I believe we shall overcome."

Immediately, we began planning the march again (we often met in the home of Dr. & Mrs. Sullivan Jackson). A federal judge placed a stay on the march because of some technicality with regard to the highway, but it was finally set for March 21, 1965.

People continued to come to Selma from everywhere. The Dallas County Voter's League provided transportation both day and night for people coming to support the march. The Voter's League owned two Volkswagen fifteen-passenger vans. The City of Selma tried to monitor the number of people coming in for the march by conducting a so-called "highway survey." When the Voter's League vans returned from the Montgomery airport, they would be stopped and the people inside counted (the vans were never stopped on the way to the airport, only from it). People continued to come until we had five thousand, then fifteen thousand, and then twenty thousand or more people coming to support and aid us in getting our voting rights.

I think about how supportive of the movement the local people were, how the coming together for a common goal did something positive for us. We worked side by side twenty-four hours a day, planning, cooking, and serving food and coffee. There was a spirit of dedication and togetherness for a common cause.

After "Bloody Sunday" and before the march on March 21, Dr. King came to Selma several times and led marches to the foot of the Edmund Pettus Bridge, but not across. The leaders of the movement chose not to cross the bridge until the federal stay was lifted. We wanted to keep our struggle in the minds of the people, but we were not willing to break any laws to do it. So the marches were planned to keep our people involved and focused on our goal as well as to remind the white folks that we were still determined to gain our voting rights.

March 21, 1965, finally came and we were prepared for our march to Montgomery. At about 1:00 p.m., Dr. King led the march from Brown Chapel A.M.E. Church. As promised, we were protected by federal troops from Selma to Montgomery. They marched before us, beside us, and behind us, and we were also given helicopter coverage and protection. Each day we would walk to a designated place to camp and have a praise service.

Finally, we made it to the steps of the Capital on Thursday morning, March 23, 1965. When we got to the Capital, we were welcomed and cheered by thousands and thousands of people. A platform had been built for the speakers of the day. Dr. King was the main speaker, and in his speech he said, "Some said we would never get here, and if we did, it would be over their dead bodies, but we made it." This was a time of joy and accomplishment. We had prayed, planned, worked and struggled to make it to this point, and we were successful.

As a result of the march, Congress passed the 1965 Voting Rights Bill. This bill did away with poll taxes, the grandfather clause, the literacy test and other devices used to prohibit black people from voting. Federal registrars were sent to assist the newly franchised voters. Black folks began to register by the hundreds and by the thousands.

Blacks began to qualify and be elected for various offices: governors, mayors, representatives, city councilpersons, school boards, commissioners, and even running for the presidency of the United States. We are now on the move, so let us keep on walking, keep on talking up the freedom way.

Some of the three hundred march participants standing between Brown Chapel and the parsonage.

Marchers lining up preparing to march from Selma to Montgomery on March 21, 1965.

Marchers finally crossing the crest of the Edmund Pettus Bridge where, two weeks earlier, many had been brutally beaten.

Federal troops were called out to protect the marchers.

Marchers leaving Brown Chapel A.M.E. Church. March 21, 1965.

VIII.

THE OTHER SIDE
JESSE JACKSON'S STORY

In a speech during a "Bloody Sunday" Commemoration service, Reverend Jesse Jackson correctly stated that Governor George Wallace successfully got the courts to issue injunctions prohibiting mass meetings in black churches, and other churches abided by the injustice imposed on them. However, Brown Chapel A.M.E. Church opened its doors to the civil rights movement. Reverend Jackson was incorrect in stating that Bishop I.H. Bonner ordered the doors of the church to be opened. Here is the true story.

One evening during the height of the civil rights movement, Bishop I.H. Bonner called and asked me to come to his home for a meeting. It was during this meeting that Bishop Bonner told me that he wanted me to close the doors of Brown Chapel to the movement.

I asked him, "Why?" Bishop Bonner responded by saying that members were calling him and saying that they wanted to have night services at the church and, because of the civil rights meetings being held at night, they could not.

I said that before the movement started we did not have night services at Brown Chapel.

Bishop Bonner said, "I want you the close the doors to the movement or I will move you from Brown Chapel."

I asked if I could speak frankly and the bishop said, "Yes."

I said, "Here you are the Bishop of the Ninth Episcopal District, and yet you are not a registered voter. I believe if you would go down to the Board of Registrars and tell them that you are the Bishop of the Ninth District, they would automatically register you. You are the president of the Bishop's Council, and living on a dirt street. You ought to be out there with us leading the marches."

Bishop Bonner listened to the comments and said, "Close the doors or I'm going to move you."

After leaving Bishop Bonner's home, I rode around for a couple of hours and finally went home. That evening I had a difficult time sleeping. I kept going over in my mind the conversation with Bishop Bonner and feeling insecure about my future at Brown Chapel. I tossed and turned the entire night.

The phone rang around 5:00 a.m. and it was Bishop Bonner. Bishop Bonner said, "Remember that little talk we had yesterday? I prayed over it and the Lord told me you were right. Whatever you need, let me know. I won't bother you and neither will anyone else." The movement went on, we continued to meet at Brown Chapel. We marched from Selma to Montgomery and eventually the civil rights voting bill was passed.

Once the 1965 Voting Right Bill was passed, Bishop Bonner called and said, "Remember the little talk we had and you told me I was not registered to vote?"

I responded, "Yes."

Bishop Bonner said, "Will you come and take me and my wife down to register to vote?"

71

I said yes and took them both, husband and wife, to become registered voters.

As part of the changes that the City of Selma was making to improve race relations, they began to pave streets in the black community. The city allowed the leaders of the movement to determine the priority in which the streets would be paved. It was during this time that Bishop Bonner called me again and said, "Remember the little talk we had, and you said I lived on a dirt street?"

"Yes," I replied.

Bishop Bonner said, "I still live on a dirt street, and I understand that you all set priority on getting streets paved. I want my street paved." Bishop Bonner's street was paved and he was happy.

I have written this so that Mrs. Betty Jean Stalling would have the rest of the story, and know that I was not sassing her grandfather, but encouraging him to actively participate in the civil rights movement.

IX.

WHAT IF THERE WERE NO BLACK FOLKS?

Courtesy of Shemita G. Sims

This is a story of a little boy named Theo, who woke up one morning and asked God, "What if there were no black people in the world?"

Well, God thought about that for a moment and then said, "Follow me around today and let's just see what it would be like if there were no black people in the world. Get dressed and we will get started."

Theo ran to his room to put on his clothes and shoes, but there were no shoes, and his clothes were all wrinkled. He looked for the iron, but when he reached for the ironing board, it was no longer there. You see, Sarah Boone, a black woman, invented the ironing board, and Jan E. Matzelling, a black man, invented the shoe lasting—or shaping—machine.

"Oh, well," said God, "go and do your hair." Theo ran into his room to comb his hair, but the comb was gone. You see, Walter

73

Sammons, a black man, invented the comb. Theo decided to just brush his hair, but the brush was gone, too. You see, Lydia O. Newman, a black female, invented the brush.

Well, he was a sight, no shoes, wrinkled clothes, hair a mess without the hair care inventions of Madam C.J. Walker—well, you get the picture. God told Theo, "Let's do the chores around the house and then take a trip to the grocery store."

Theo's job was to sweep the floor. He swept and swept and swept. When he reached for the dustpan, it was not there. You see, Lloyd P. Ray, a black man, invented the dustpan. So he swept his pile of dirt over in the corner and left it there. He then decided to mop the floor, but the mop was gone. You see, Thomas W. Stewart, a black man, invented the mop.

Theo thought to himself, "I'm not having any luck."

"Well, son," God said, "we should wash the clothes and prepare a list for the grocery store." When he was finished, Theo went to place the clothes in the dryer, but it was not there. You see, George T. Samon, a black man, invented the clothes dryer.

Theo got a pencil and some paper to prepare the list for the market, but noticed that the pencil lead was broken, and he couldn't sharpen it because John Love, a black man, invented the pencil sharpener. He reached for a pen, but it was not there because William Purvis, a black man, invented the fountain pen. As a matter of fact, Lee Burridge invented the typewriting machine, and W.A. Lavette a printing press. They were both Blacks.

So they decided to head out to the market. Well, when Theo opened the door, he noticed the grass was as high as he was tall. You see, the lawnmower was invented by John Burr, a black man.

They made their way over to the car and found that it just wouldn't go. You see, Robert Spikes, a black man, invented the automatic gear shift, and Joseph Gammel invented the supercharge system for internal combustion engines.

They noticed that the few cars that were moving were running into each other and having wrecks because there were no traffic signals. You see, Garrett A. Morgan, a black man, invented the traffic light.

Well, it was getting late, so they walked to the market, got their groceries, and returned home. Just when they were about to put away the milk, eggs, and butter, they noticed the refrigerator was gone. You see, John Standard, a black man, invented the refrigerator. So they put the food on the counter.

By this time, they noticed it was getting mighty cold. Theo went to turn up the heat, and what do you know, Alive Parker, a black female, invented the heating furnace. Even in the summertime they would have been out of luck because Frederick Jones, a black man, invented the air conditioner.

It was almost time for Theo's father to arrive home. He usually took the bus, but there was no bus because its precursor was the electric trolley, invented by another black man, Elbert T. Robinson. Theo's father usually took the elevator from his office on the twentieth floor, but there was no elevator, because Alexander Miles, a black man, invented the elevator. He usually dropped off the office mail at a nearby mailbox, but it was no longer there because Philip Downing, a black man, invented the letter drop mailbox and William Barry invented the postmarking and canceling machine.

Theo sat at the kitchen table with his head in his hands. When his father arrived, he asked, "Why are you sitting in the dark?"

"Why?" Because Lewis Howard Latimer, a black man, invented the filament within the light bulb.

Theo quickly learned what it would be like if there were no black people in the world.

Charles Drew, a black scientist, found a way to preserve and store blood, which led to his starting the world's first blood bank.

Dr. Daniel Hale Williams, a black doctor, was the first to perform open heart surgery.

So if you wonder, like Theo, where would we be without Blacks, it's pretty plain to see we could very well still be in the dark.

X

CITATION FROM DR. HOWARD D. GREGG

President of Daniel Payne College

It is felt by many that the antagonistic attitude of Alabama officials after the Supreme Court decision of 1954 caused considerable turmoil and violence in the state. How much they contributed to the animosity and backlash on a national scale is interesting but is not a part of this study. The governor of Alabama did, however, as promised to the state, carry out his intentions in Tuscalosa, Alabama, the home of the University of Alabama. Judge Seymour H. Lynne, acting upon a plea from the Justice Department, did forbid the governor from physically interposing his person to block the Negroes from entering the University of Alabama. He extended the prohibition to include all persons in consort with the governor. Judge Lynne concluded his ruling with this personal note:

"May it be forgiven if this court makes use of the personal pronoun for the first time in a written opinion. I love the people of Alabama. I know that many of both races are troubled and like Jonah of old, are "angry even unto death" as a result to distortions of affairs within this state practiced in the name of segregationalism.

"My prayer is that all of our people, in keeping with our finest traditions, will join in the resolution that law and order will be maintained, both in Tuscaloosa and in Huntsville."

Speaking on a state-wide television program after this ruling by Judge Lynne, the governor stated that he might defy the court order and block the entrance of Negro students to the University of Alabama. "I will not let you down," said the governor.

To a careful observer, it would appear that the state was headed for a type of violence that would make the rioting eight years earlier when Arthurine Lucy attempted to enroll look like a Sunday school picnic. More than three thousand army troops were marshaled at strategic places in Alabama. The governor ordered five hundred more military police units to prepare to move into the area on Sunday during the night. There were also some four-hundred-twenty-five State troopers already in the area and about four hundred government revenue agents and some other units assigned to the area. Monday, June 10, it was reported that President Kennedy sent the governor a message asking him not to stand in the door as he promised in his campaign pledge. The governor, it is said, ignored the message and did stand in the door to block the passing of Negro students. President John F. Kennedy federalized the National Guard, and the students were admitted unmolested after several exchanges of words.

One of the students who faced the governor in this confrontation was twenty-year-old Vivian Malone of Mobile,

Alabama. Ms. Malone was a member of Emanuel A.M.E. Church in Mobile. She was the first Negro graduate of the University of Alabama. This young lady certainly deserves the plaudits of the entire world, since it required courage and determination to seek equality of treatment under such circumstances. She was indeed carrying out the philosophy of Richard Allen and the spirit of the A.M.E. church.

It would seem that the lesson learned in Alabama would have taught Mississippi that defiance would not pay. This was not the case, however. Mississippi after the Supreme Court decision of 1954 actually persisted in defiance of the law of the land. In May, 1961, when James Meredith filed suit in the District Court for Southern Mississippi saying he had been denied admission to the University of Mississippi because he was a Negro, his plea attracted national attention. When he finally was permitted to enter after many legal battles, a riot started, which lasted more than fifteen hours and left two dead and many injured. James Meredith finished as the first Negro graduate of the University of Mississippi, upholding the Supreme Court decision of 1954. Sporadic incidents of violence occurred in both Mississippi and Alabama for perhaps five years, with very little justice shown in prosecuting those who molested Negroes.

In Selma, Alabama, tension was extremely high and violence in the streets—even murder—was almost commonplace. A white minister from Boston, Reverend James Reeb, was murdered in the street just as leaders of the Southern Christian Leadership Conference were planning a march from Selma to Montgomery. It is reported that Bishop Bonner of the A.M.E. church, who was presiding over the Ninth Episcopal District, gave substantial funds to aid in the early preparation for the march. I am grateful to acknowledge that I, too, was recognized for my efforts in the Selma civil rights movement. I am a graduate of the college and seminary of Daniel Payne College, and, because of my stand in the Selma to Montgomery march, the college called me back and conferred upon me the honorary Doctor of Divinity degree. A part of the citation given to me is as follows:

> Reverend Prinic H. Lewis, Pastor of Brown Chapel A.M.E. Church, because you were courageous enough to turn your entire church over to the marchers of the Selma to Montgomery march; because this march aided in crystallizing sentiment for the passage of subsequent Civil Rights legislation, for the benefit of Negroes; because of your stand in carrying out the philosophy of Richard Allen in going up against entrenched evil and unfair treatment against Negroes regardless of the strength of the opposition; because you have sacrificed and struggled risking bodily harm and danger and even death to carry forward principles which you believe embrace the philosophy of your church, your college is honored to call you back and confer upon you this honorary degree, Doctor of Divinity.

It is useless to say that the fact that hundreds slept in the Brown Chapel A.M.E. Church was not only costly but damaging to the church as well. But I considered that it was my duty to carry out the philosophy of Richard Allen, and the church did not complain about the decision to use both the building and the parsonage. My task was to educate local people to see the principles involved, and to get them to aid me in taking a stand against entrenched wrong regardless of cost. Perhaps our connectional A.M.E. church lost a golden opportunity to dramatize the sacrifices made by all of us, including the congregation of Brown Chapel A.M.E. Church in Selma, Alabama. The laymen of the A.M.E. church, and Mr. J.D. Wilham, president, voted to give one thousand dollars to Brown Chapel A.M.E. Church at its meeting in New Orleans, Louisiana, in 1967. I know of no other group who has voted to send us funds, although there may have been others.

XI.

MEMBERS OF THE GROUND CREW

As I sat in the Brown Chapel Church, March 5, 2000, and listened to Congressman John Lewis talk about "Bloody Sunday of 1965," my mind went back to the days when I was pastoring Brown Chapel Church. I was reminded of a true story told by the late Reverend J.T.L Dandridge, who also pastored Brown Chapel Church, from 1939-1948. He said to me, "Reverend Lewis, don't ever say anything from the pulpit that you don't want to get back downtown to the white folks." Then he went on to tell me of an incident that happened before he became the pastor of Brown Chapel. He quoted Reverend Hughes, who said from the pulpit, ". . .that people who are day laborers and maids need to ask their boss for minimum wages and social security, which is the law."

And of course, it got back downtown that he had informed his parishioners of this pertinent information. A mob was formed and started out after Reverend Hughes. A Reverend Carter went to the parsonage, got Reverend Hughes and drove him out East Selma on a dusty road. In the midst of all this dust, Reverend

Hughes jumped out of the car and laid down in a ditch. The mob passed him by. The mob caught up with Reverend Carter, and they dragged him out of the car and took him to a tree.

A white woman came by and asked, "What y'all doing to that nigger? I know him and can speak for him." So they let him go. Reverend Hughes and Reverend Carter left Alabama and ended up in New York.

This was not a fairy tale. This actually happened. Knowing that story, I still opened the doors of Brown Chapel African Methodist Episcopal Church.

As I sat there and reflected upon the past, I was reminded again of an incident that happened in 1965. After the movement was on its way, I was invited to Chicago to speak at a rally. I flew from Montgomery to Atlanta. When I got to Atlanta and boarded the plane for Chicago, we taxied out on the runway two, three times. Each time the pilot had to go back and let the mechanics work on the plane. The last time we taxied out, we finally became airborne. We were flying at an attitude of 30,000 or 40,000 feet at a speed of more than 600 miles per hour. The seat belt sign went off and the flight attendants started serving dinner, and all of us were sitting there eating this delicious steak dinner. The attendants were doing their job, the pilots were in their place. My mind went back to the ground crew, who made the flight possible. As I sat listening to those in high places, my mind went back to members of the ground crew for civil rights. Had it not been for the ground crew, we would not have been successful in the movement.

Some members of the ground crew are listed below:

Mrs. Classic Abbott
Mrs. Mary Eliza Acoff
Mr. Rathn Acoff
Mrs. Aiken

M.W. Akins
Mrs. Bearice Albritton
Joe Albritton
Rosa Ales

Mrs. Daisy Alexander
Mr. Joe Allen
Miss Annie Pearl Allen
Miss Beatrice Allen
Miss Mabel Allen
Reverend L.L. Anderson
Mattie Lee Anderson
Mrs. Lizia Anderson
Nancy Anderson
Mrs. P.D. Anderson
P.L. Anderson
Mrs. Rebecca Anderson
Mrs. Rosie Anderson
Mrs. Susita Anderson
Miss W.M. Anderson
Elbert Arnold
Herman Arnold
Miss Mary Alice Atury
Sylvester Austin
Mrs. Mattie Babcock
Willie King Bady
Mrs. Ann Bailey
Nelacy Bailey
Virgil Ballet
Abraham L. Banks
Julia Banks
Mrs. Ardie Barefield
Mrs. Eddie Barefield
Mrs. Cennie Barge
Mrs. Pauline H. Barge
Willie Barlow
Shirley Barnes
Mrs. Sallie M. Barnett
James Bates
Miss Ruby L. Battle

Mrs. August Bell Bean
Ernest Beckham
Johnnie Bell
Mrs. Johnnie Mae Bell
Mrs. Ella Lee Belvins
James Bender
James M. Bender
Jessie L. Benefield
Mrs. Sarah Benjamin
Annie Bennett
Carrie Bennett
Robert Bennett
Mrs. Willie A. Bennett
Mrs. Wueen Bennett
Mrs. Ernestine Bettis
Mrs. Rosie Bishop
Stanford Black
Joann Blackmon
Ulysses Blackmon
James Blevin
Ben Blevins
Mrs. Ella Lee Blevins
Mrs. Louise Blevins
Mrs. Lucile Blevins
Mr. T.H. Blevins
Mary Bolding
Maxie Bonner
Mrs. Vera Booker
Mrs. Alberta Bossie
Mrs. Elsie Boyd
Mrs. Tommie Boyd
Mrs. Eula Boykins
Martha Boykins
Phillip Boykins
Reverend E.M. Bradford

Dora Brantley
Mrs. Pauline Brantley
Mrs. Bettie Bratton
Mrs. Alma Brazier
Mr. Napoleon Brazier
William L. Brentley
Mrs. Centa Brewer
Mrs. Emma Brewer
Butler Brigg
Mrs. Lucy Brock
Mrs. Bernice N. Brooks
Ernest Brooks
Leonard Brooks
Mrs. Momie Brooks
Miss R.J. Brooks
Mrs. Rita Brooks
Alberta Browder
Mrs. Cecile Browder
Alex Brown
Mrs. Crandell C. Brown
Mrs. E.H. Brown
Mrs. Elsie Brown
Miss Hettie Brown
Reverend J.F. Brown
Mrs. L.R. Brown
Mrs. Maggie Brown
Mamie R. Brown
Mrs. Myrtle H. Brown
Mrs. Ruth Brown
Sarah Brown
Mrs. Abell Bryant
Mrs. Rita Bryant
Dan Bryd
Mary Buchanan
Cetonia Buford

Clara Buford
Mrs. H.J. Buford
Mrs. Marie Bullard
Mrs. W.M. Bumstead
Ed Burden
Rosia Burrell
A.D. Bush
Dora Butler
Earley Butler
Emily Butler
Mrs. Channey Caffey
Mrs. Ada Bell Calhoun
Verdell Calhoun
Miss Virginia Calhoun
Mrs James Calhoune
Merry Calhoune
Mrs. Bertha Lee Callens
James Callens Sr
Janie Callens
Raymond Callens
Leroy Callin
Mary Campbell
Ora Bell Carr
Kent Wayne Carrington
Mrs. C.J. Carter
Ella Carter
Miss Dorothy D. Carter
Ernest Carter
Mrs. M.P. Cater
Thomas N. Cater
Mrs. Rosetta Caver
Miss Willie Mae Caver
Reverend Issac J. Ceasar
Emma Chancey
Mrs. Willie B. Channey

Leon Cheese
Mrs. P.B. Cheese
Miss Dorothy Cherry
Mrs. Minnie Cherry
Helen Chestnut
Mr. & Mrs. Mallory Chestnut
Mrs. Lula Christian
Mrs. Essie Clark
Patricia Clark
Mrs. Rosie Clark
Mrs. Gertrude Clay
William Cleaven
C.L. Cleveland
Mrs. R.P. Cleveland
Will Coats
Mrs. Jumanita Coats
Mrs. Laura Coker
Henry Cole
Mrs. Pauline Cole
Richard Cole Jr
Mrs. Eloise Coleman
Mrs. Estella Coleman
Reverend G.C. Coleman
Mrs. Mary Coleman
Robert Coleman
Mrs. Susie Coleman
Addie F. Collins
Mrs. Francis Collins
Mr. Jessie Collins
Mrs. Ovetta Collins
Velma Collins
Dollie Cook
Elizabeth Cook
W.L. Cooper
Mrs. Lelia Cooper

Miss Mary Counsel
Mrs. Inez Courtland
Curtis S. Cowan
Ella Mae Craig
Lorenza M. Craig
Reverend O. Craig
Miss Rosie Mae Craig
Mrs. S.C. Craig
Mrs. Sarah M. Craig
Thomas Craig
W.C.R. Craig
Mrs Willie Dean Craig
Zola Mae Craig
Willie J. Crawford
Mr. & Mrs. Johnny Crear
James Crumb
Mr. Louise Culpepper
Jesse Cunningham
Mrs. Gertrude Cunningham
Miss Mary Cunningham
Mr. Clanton Curtis
Mrs. Viola Curtis
Mrs. Emma Daniels
Mary Alice Danwell
Mrs. Rebecca P. Danwell
L.W. Danzy
Eugene Darton
Annie Davis
Annie Mae Davis
Mrs. Bertha Davis
Charles E. Davis
Mrs. Crabelle Davis
Miss Eunice Davis
Ezelle Davis
Hester Davis

John H. Davis
Johnny Davis
Mrs. Irene Davis
Mrs. Juliet C. Davis
Mrs. Lenner Davis
Mrs. Lillie Bell Davis
Mrs. Lucy B. Davis
Miss Malerie Davis
Olie Mae Davis
Sam Davis
Mrs. Shirley Marie Davis
Houser Dawson
Mrs. Margaret Dawson
Mrs. Clara Day
Nona N. Day
Mrs. Charlotte DeLoach
Miss Estella DeLoach
Mrs. Aggie M. Dixon
Miss Bessie G. Dixon
Mrs. Eleanor Dixon
Mamie Dorton
Willie Doss
Mrs. Willie Mae Doss
Mrs. Geneva Douglas
Mattie M. Douglas
E.L. Doyle
Mrs. Eddie Mae DuBose
Mrs. Love Dubose
Love Lou DuBose
Mrs. Rosa Dudley
Mrs. Josephine Dukes
John Duncan
J. Estelle Dunham
Mrs. Leola Y. DuRant
A.J. Durgan

Mrs. Ira H. Durgan
Mrs. Bessie S. Durry
Buhl Durry
John Durry
J.L. Ealy
Miss Lenora A. Eaton
Mrs. Ella Edward
Mrs. E.B. Edwards
Eulean Edwards
Mrs. Lela Edwards
Mrs. Pertie Edwards
Mrs. Essie Eilliams
Mrs. Estella Ellis
Mrs. Ola Mae Ellis
Mr. Jerry Etheridge
Mr. Mitchell Etheridge
Ed Evans
Mrs. Mabel Evans
Miss O'Lillian Evans
W.G. Evans
Ester Failes
Mr. and Mrs. Clifton Fain
John Feggins
Mrs. J.P. Finley
Mrs. Roszene Fisher
N.C. Flakes
Mrs. Bessie M. Ford
Miss Estella Ford
Mr. James Ford
Mrs. James Ford
William Fortune
Clifford Foster
Mrs. James Foster
Lena Foster
Mrs. Lila Foster

Mrs. Lula Mae Foster
Marie Foster
Mr. Johnnie Franklin
L. Franklin
Mrs. Mable Franklin
Ethel L. French
Ora Bell Fulford
Mrs. Julia M. Fullenwilden
Eliza Fuller
Mrs. Eva Fuller
Reverend W.F. Fuller
Bertharine Furlow
Lee Gadden
Olicer Gales Jr
Reverend G.D. Gallaway
Mrs. D.L. Gardner
Oneather Garrett
Mr. Will Gary
Mary George
Elvira Gibson
Isaac Benjamin Gibson
James E. Gildersleeves
Mrs. L.B. Gildersleeve
Susie Giles
Mattie Gill
Marion Gillersleeve
Mrs. Mildred Givan
Mr. & Mrs. Lorell Givhan
Miss Mary Givhan
Will Gloss
Mrs. Annie Mae Glover
Joseph Glover
Mrs. R.G. Gohmer
Mr. John H. Goldsby
Mrs. Ora Mae Goldsby

Thomas Goldsby
Michel Goods
Queen Goods
Florence Goodwin
Mrs. Laura Goodwin
Mrs. S.H. Goodwin
Charles Gordon
Mrs. Grace Gordon
Miss Laura Mae Gordon
Mrs. Susie Gordon
Mrs. Dissie Gould
Isom Gould
Wally M. Graham
Mrs. Allie Grayson
Annie Mae Grayson
Edward Grayson
Elizes P. Grayson
Mrs. Carrie Green
Clara Green
Mrs. James Green
Johnny Green
Lewis Green
Mrs. Lillie M. Green
Henry Gregg Jr
Mrs. Johnnie Lee Grice
Mrs. Margie Grice
Mrs. F.D. Griffin
Jessie James Griffin
Mr. Julius Griffin
Mrs. Lillie Mae Griffin
Mrs. Lula Griffin
Mrs. M.G. Griffin
N.H. Griffin
Mrs. Sarah Griffin
Mattie Grimes

Rosie Lee Grimes
Willie Grimes
J. Gullett
Mrs. L.T. Gulley
James Gutheridge
Mrs. Mellnee Guthridge
Mrs. Hester Hale
Mrs. Charlotte H. Hall
Mrs. Clarence Hall
James Hall
Mrs. Lillie Pearl Hall
Mrs. Myrtlene Hall
John Hamler
Arnettie Hampton
Lottie Hampton
Janie Mack Hardie
Mrs. Nancy Hardie
Miss V. Hardwick
Carrie Mae Hardy
Henry Hardy
John Hardy
Mrs. Rose Hardy
Sallie Hardy
Tommie Hardy
Mrs. Dora A. Harper
Celeope B. Harrell
Lillie B. Harrell
Mrs. Alice Harris
Annie Grace Harris
Charles Harris III
Clarence Harris
Mrs. E.S. Harris
George Harris
Mrs. Julia Harris
Mrs. K.W. Harris

Mrs. Kathleen Harris
Ola B. Harris
Willie Harris
Reverend T.R. Harris
Celister Harrison Jr
Mrs. Eula Harrison
Vivian Harrison
Willie Harrison
Inez Harvey
Mrs. Sylvia Hasberry
Rev. & Mrs. M.S. Hasty
Mr. E.L. Hatch
Mrs. Mary Hatcher
Carrie Hatchett
A.G. Hatchett
Mrs. Dorothy Hayes
Frances Hayes
Irene Hayes
Miss Juliet Hayes
Mrs. Laura Hayes
Mrs. E. Haywood
Mrs. Minnie Hazens
Mrs. Josey B. Henry
Mrs. Leatha Hester
Mrs. Willine Hickman
Mrs. Amanda Hicks
Mrs. Inez Hicks
Claude Hilberth
Ben Hill
Mrs. Lucy Hill
Timothy Hill
Annie M. Hills
James Hines
Sophronia Hines
Mrs. Annie W. Hogan

Lee R. Hogan
McKinley Hogan
Louise Holeman
Mr. Junior Holiday
A.P. Hollman
Mrs. Ada Hollman
Mrs. Mary Holloway
Mrs. Ceola Holmes
Mr. H.H. Holmes
H.J. Holmes
Mrs. Harriet M. Holmes
Mr. Corine Home
Sam Hopkins Sr
Mrs. Mary Hopkins
Mrs. Annie Mae Hopkins
Mrs. Lucy P. Hopson
Mrs. Allie Hosea
George Hosea
Gertrude Hosea
Mary L. Hosy
Jean Hoszies
Mrs. Bertha M. Houser
Britt M. Houser
Mrs. Carrie L. Houser
John Houser
Willie Houston
Anna Howard
Reverend E.M. Howard
Mrs. Jessie Howard
Miss Mamie L. Howard
Mrs. Mollie Howard
Mrs. Leroy Howard
Charles T. Huckabee
Percy Huckabee
Mrs. Ethel Hudson

Mrs. Frances Hudson
Mrs. Hattie J. Hudson
Mr. Henry Hudson
Melvin Hudson
William Hudson
Mrs. Dorthea T. Huggins
Lawrence F. Huggins
Tommie Hunt
Alice Hunter
Bertha Hunter
Reverend J.D. Hunter
Levi Hunter
Louis Hunter
Lue Ellen Hunter
Mrs. Mamie Hunter
Martha Hunter
William Hunter
Johnson Hutchins
Barnell Ingram
Miss Irma Irby
Mrs. Louise Irby
Mrs. V.L. Irby
Mrs. Gracie Ivery
Eugene Ivory
Amellia Jackson
Mrs. Aridelia Jackson
Beatrice Jackson
Birdie Jackson
Eddie N. Jackson
Mrs. Elizabeth Jackson
Miss Era Dean M. Jackson
Mrs. Estella Jackson
Mrs. Ethel H. Jackson
Henry Jackson
Mrs. Jean Jackson

Leala Jackson

Leola Jackson

Miss Lillie B. Jackson

Lorena Jackson

Lula Mae Jackson

Mark Jackson

Mrs. Mary Jackson

Miss O. Jackson

O.T. Jackson

Rebecca Jackson

Rosie Lee Jackson

Dr. S. Jackson

Mrs. Nettie B. James

Mrs. Mamervia Jarden

Alice Jemison

Rosa Jiles

Mrs. Beatrice Johnson

Miss Bessie Johnson

Mrs. Billie S. Johnson

Mrs. Bobby Johnson

Catherine Johnson

Dorothy Johnson

Mr. & Mrs. E. Johnson

Mrs. Ella Mae Johnson

Ernestine Johnson

George Johnson

Jesse Johnson

Jessie Lee Johnson

Joe Lewis Johnson

Mrs. Marie Johnson

Norma Johnson

Miss Sadie Johnson

Miss Tommie Johnson

Miss Willie Mae Johnson

Wise Johnson

Annie M. Jones

Calvin Jones

Mrs. Carrie S. Jones

Mrs. Carrie L. Jones

Mrs. Charlotte Jones

Mr. Dan L. Jones

Dock Jones Jr

E.O. Jones

Ernest L. Jones

Ethel S. Jones

Mrs. Eulalie Jones

Flossie Mae Jones

H. James Jones

Homer Jones

Howard Jones

Miss Irene Jones

J.M. Jones

James A. Jones

Mrs. Kathlene Jones

Louise Jones

Mrs. Lula M. Jones

Mrs. M.L. Jones

Mrs. Mary E. Jones

Mrs. Mary Jane Jones

Mrs. Mary J. Jones

Miss Matilda Jones

Mrs. Odessa Jones

Ola B. Jones

Mrs. R. Jones

Mrs. Yvonne C. Jones

Mrs. Jimmie Kelley

Cornelia Kelly

Mrs. Daisy Mae Kelly

Mrs. Rosie Kelly

Reverend W.M. Kemp

Mrs. F. Kent
Mrs. Bessie Killingsworth
Dock Killingsworth
Mrs. Ella Kimber
Miss Minnie Kimber
Miss Blanche Kimbrough
J.C. Kimbrough
Eddie King
Mrs. Ella M. King
Etta Bell King
Mrs. G. King
Mrs. Mary King
Mrs. Mattie King
Willie L. King
Nathaniel Kirksey
Mrs. Willie Mae Kirksey
Mrs. Hattie Kith
Mrs. Annie B. Ladd
Mrs. LeGrande Lamar
Mrs. Rosetta Lanier
Theresa LaShore
Mrs. Annie Law
Mrs. Bessie Law
Mrs. Betty Law
Mrs. Daisy Law
Mr. Eary Law
Mrs. Mattie Law
Frankie Mae Lawyer
Mrs. Vashti LeaShore
Mrs. Annie L. Lee
Mrs. Carlean Lee
Claurs Lee
James Lee
Mrs. Rachel Lee
Mrs. York Lee Sr

Mrs. Minnie T. Lett
Alex Lewis
Mrs. Alice G. Lewis
Annie Lewis
John Lewis
Lela Mae Lewis
Mrs. Mabel Lewis
Mrs. Mary Lewis
Morgan Lewis
Reverend P.H. Lewis
Mrs. Rosa Mae Lewis
Mrs. Sallie Lewis
Sam Lewis
Addie Lilly
P.L. Lindsey
Mrs. Ruth Lindsey
Carl Lockett
Mrs. Alberta Lords
Mrs. Susie Mae Love
Mrs. Ethel Lundy
Miss Hettie Lundy
Sarah Lylcs
Doris Lynn
Annie Lee Mack
Hattie Mack
Judy Mack
Mrs. G.D. Maddox
Mrs. Carrie Bell Manuel
Miss Elizabeth J. Manuel
Lucy Marshall
Mrs. Mary Marshall
Columbus Martin
Dorothy L. Martin
Fannie Martin
Mrs. Geneva Martin

Mrs. Lillie Martin
Mary Martin
Mrs. Matilda Martin
Napoleon Martin
Mr. Ronnie Martin
Miss Addie Martinear
Mr. David Martinear
Miss Leola Martinear
Daniel Mason
Mrs. Marva P. Mason
Mrs. C. Belle Matthews
Johnny Mathews
Calvin P. Maze
Shirley McCaskey
Elvira McCastar
George McClain
Mrs. Eddie McConnell
James McCord
Mrs. Mary E. McCord
Miss Ethel McCorvey
William McCorvey
Andrew McDaniel
Ethel McDole
Murrie Lee McDole
Reverend R.C. McElroy
John McGee
Mrs. Rosa McGee
Ada Bell McGhee, N.L.
Charles I. McGhee
Miss Gladys B. McGrue
Lucy McGrue
Miss Laura McGuire
W. Young Wmma McLin
Mrs. Bety McMillan
Mrs. Fannie McMillan

Mrs. Rosa McMillan
Mrs. Annie McNeal
David McNeill Jr
Mrs. Annie McQueen
Samuel L. McWilliams
Burnette F. Mealing
Mrs. Ada B. Melton
Mrs. Rosie Todd Melton
C.F. Merritt
Mrs. Evelyn H. Merritt
Mrs. Bertha Miles
Mary Ann Miles
R.D. Miles
Mr. Bernice Miller
Josie Jean Miller
Lewis Miller
Mrs. Dorothy M. Milton
Mary Minniefield
Mrs. Earlene Minor
Mrs. Lola B. Miree
Alfred Mitchell
Eddie Lee Mitchell
George Mitchell
Henry Mitchell
Hollis Mitchell
J.S. Mitchell
Joe Mitchell
Rev. Leonard R. Mitchell
Lou Alice Mitchell
Lucy Mitchell
Rose Mitchell
Mrs. Thelma Mitchell
Theodore Mitchell
Mrs. Viola Mitchell
Mrs. Earlene Mixon

Mrs. Mary Ann Mixon
Mrs. Viola Mixon
Mrs. Annie W. Molette
Lernice Molette
Paul Molette
Frank Montgomery
Alphones Moore
Mrs. Annie L. Moore
Mrs. Bama Moore
D.M. Moore
Mrs. Eddie Mae Moore
Mrs. G.G.S. Moore
Herman Moore
James Moore
Mr. L.D. Moore
Mrs. Margaret J. Moore
Miss Mary Louise Moore
Mrs. Mary Moore
Mr. Mattie Moore
T. Moore Jr
Mrs. Rosa Moorer
Mrs. Lillie Mae Morgan
Mr. Lucy Morgan
Mr. Piad Morgan
James Morrow
Mrs. E.K. Morton
Mrs. E.M. Morton
Julie Mosley
Mrs. Alberta G. Moss
Charles (Chas.) A. Moss
E.L.D. Moss
Miss Sophronia Moss
Thomas M. Moss
Mrs. Mary Moton
Mrs. Rose Moton

F.C. Mumford Jr
H.C. Munford Jr
Bruce Murphy
Ms. Clementine Murphy
Mrs. Irene Murphy
James Murray
Mrs. James Murray
Willie Murray
Catherine Murry
Leola Nelson
Mack Nelson
Mrs. Ethylene J. Nettles
Willie F. Nettles
Mr. Robert J. Newell
Miss Ruth Nunn
Pauline Oden
Mrs. Susie Oden
Mrs. Edna B. Olds
Joe Oliver
Miss Esther M. Owens
Wuencie Paldin
G.G. Palmore
Annie M. Parker
Reverend B.B. Parker
Mrs. Mary Parker
Miss Mattie Lee Parker
McCeauly Parker
Mrs. Ethel Parnell
Mrs. Polly Parnell
Mrs. A.S. Parrish
Mrs. Fannie Parrish
Miss Lula S. Parrish
Mrs. Eddie Patterson
Reverend J.H. Patterson
Virginia Patterson

Mrs. Quincia Pauldin
Jack Payne
Mrs. Ida Mae Pearl
John Pearl
Mrs. Eddie L. Peeples
Miss Minnie L. Peggins
Mrs. Carlena Peoples
Mrs. Lucy Pepper
James Perkins
Maggie Perkins
Mrs. Ola Mae Perkins
Mrs. Rita S. Perkins
Mrs. A.D. Perry
Robert J. Perry
Betty L. Peterson
Emma L. Peterson
Mrs. Josephine Peterson
Mrs. Fannie Pettaway
Mrs. Willie Pettaway
Mrs. Amy L. Petteway
Cora Petteway
Walter Pharr
Mrs. A. Phillips
Mrs. D.R. Phillips
Mrs. Susie Phillips
Mrs. Louvenia Pickets
Mrs. Katherine Pledger
Celeope B. Pollnitz
Cleophus Pollnitz
Ordell Pollnitz
Joe Nathan Pollnitz
Walter Pollnitz
Rhoda Pompoy
Mrs. Lucy Pope
Mrs. Verdell Porta

Mrs. Gertrude Porter
Dorth Portis
Joann Portis
Miss Rose Lee Portis
Rose Be Powell
Mrs. Mary L. Pressey
Shirley R. Pressley
James Preston
Flora Prevo
Mrs. Johnnie Prevo
Richard Price
Eugene Prichett
Mr. Arthor Lewis Prince
Miss D. Prince
Mrs. Gertrude Prince
Mr. Tommie Prince
Mrs. A.B. Pritchett
Minnie Pugh
Mrs. Annie L. Pullom
Miss Zettie Purifoy
Mrs. Lorrean Rainey
Fred Ramsey
Ike Ransom
Mrs. Lizzie Ransom
Willie Ray
Roberta Rayford
Rosetta Rayford
Mrs. Roxie Rayford
Dorrie Reed
Mrs. Lula Reed
Sam Reed
Uylesses Reed
Mrs. Alline C. Reese
Ceola Reese
Emma T. Reese

F.D. Reese
Lue Dell Reese
Mary Reese
Mrs. Mellanee Reese
Willie L. Reese
Beatrice Reide
Mrs. Rosa B. Rembert
Will Rembert
Mrs. Onnie Reynolds
Mrs. Pauline J. Reynolds
Annie B. Rhodes
Frank Rhodes
Mrs. Johnna E. Rhodes
Solomon Rhodes
Eddie Pearl Rice
Mrs. Ethel Richardson
Hillis Richardson
Miss Lillie B. Richardson
Miss Murene Richardson
Mrs. N.M. Richardson
Mrs. Rosie L. Richardson
Dora Ritten
Mrs. Bernice Rivers
Clara V. Rivers
Sadie Robbins
Mrs. Callie Roberson
Georgia Roberts
Mrs. Thos. L. Robertson
Mrs. Annie Robinson
Mrs. Evie Robinson
George Robinson
James Robinson
Joe Robinson
Mrs. Mabel D. Robinson
Mrs. Patricia Robinson

Jannie Rodgers
Annie Rogers
Cecil Rogers
Elijah Rogers
Mrs. Georgia Rogers
Mrs. Mary Rogers
Miss Naomi Rogers
Mrs. Roberta Rogers
Miss Rozene Rogers
Mrs. Julia M. Rogney
Doris Roller
Mrs. Willie A. Roscoes
Mrs. Addie Ross
Mrs. Calaria Ross
Mrs. Josephine Rudolph
Mrs. Tena B. Rudolph
Jamie Ruffin
Johnnie Ruffin
Mrs. Catherine Russell
Jessie (Gussie) Russell
Mrs. Maeola Russell
Mary Ola Russell
Eugene Rutledge
Mrs. F.E. Rutledge
Mr. & Mrs. Leonard D.
    Rutledge Sr
Willie Rutledge
Mrs. Ola Sample
Mrs. Carrie P. Sanders
Mrs. Emma Sanders
Miss Josephine Sanders
Mrs. Willie Sanders
Mrs. Carrie P. Savage
Mrs. Estella Savage
Alene Scott

C.D. Scott II
J.H. Scott
Lewis Scott
Lottie Scott
Mrs. Rosa Scott
Mrs. Stewardie Scott
Mrs. Mamie Nell Seals
Sarah Mae Seals
Laura Seay
Miss J.R. Sewell
Manie Sewell
Mrs. Marzella Sewell
Elnora Shannon
Mr. Henry Shannon Jr
Mr. Henry Shannon Sr
Mrs. Lillie Bell Shannon
James N. Sharp
Mrs. Lula Sharp
Mrs. Ovetta Sharp
Miss Rosie Sharp
Grace Shaw
Ulysses Shortridge
Mrs. Dora Simmons
Mrs. Doris Simon
Autherine Simpson
Adelaide Sims
John Sims
S. Sgt. Henry L. Singleton
Mrs. Dorothy Smiley
Miss Earlene Smiley
Josephine Smiley
Alice Smith
Mrs. Annie Lee Smith
Annie Marie Smith
Arthur Smith

Ben Smith
Mrs. Carrie M. Smith
Clanton Smith
Mrs. E.S. Smith
Mrs. Elizabeth D. Smith
Mr. & Mrs. Frank Smith
Mrs. Garlena Smith
George Smith Jr
Mr. & Mrs. H.D. Smith Jr
Mrs. Hattie Smith
Henry Smith
Mrs. Irene Smith
J.M. Smith
Joseph Smith
Mrs. Juanita Smith
Laurdell Smith
Mrs. M.E. Smith
Matthew Smith
Mattie Smith
Ottis Smith
Mrs. Pauldao Smith
Mrs. Rebecca J. Smith
Ruby Smith
Mrs. S.E. Smith
Samuel Lee Smith
Mrs. Sarah Smith
Theodore Smith
Mrs. Willie Smith
Mrs. Willie Mae Smith
Mrs. Ivie Snow
Mrs. Leola Southall
Minnie B. Square
Mrs. Willie M. Squire
Mrs. Ada Stallworth
Mrs. Dorothy Stallworth

John E. Stallworth
Mamie Stallworth
Mrs. Trudie Standberry
Gloria Stanford
Andrew Steele
Janita Steele
Jim Steele
Lottie LeSure Steele
Mathew Steele
Robert Stephson
Aliston Stevenson
Edrice Stevenson
Henry Stevenson
Herbert Stevenson
Lillie Mae Stevenson
Mary Stevenson
Mr. Alonza Stewart
Mrs. Geneva Stewart
Mrs. T.L. Stewart
Mrs. Lottie Stockman
Anita Strong
Mrs. Claudia Strong
Georgia Ann Strong
Joseph Strong
Mrs. Jennie Lee Strong
Mrs. Mary Strong
Nancy Lee Strong
Andy Struggs
Minnie Lee Struggs
Ms. Quentella Sturdivant
C. Sullivan
Mrs. George C. Suttles
Mrs. Luke Bell Suttles
Mrs. Ovetta Suttles
Mrs. Laurena A. Sutton

W.R. Sutton Sr
Mrs. Estella Swan
Geanette Sykles
Emmett Tabb
Leroy Tabb Sr
Mrs. Rebecca Tabb
Miss Rosie Tabb
W.J. Taggert
Mrs. Clara A. Tait
Mrs. Odessa Tait
Gussie Tarrance
Fred Tate
Mrs. Ira Mae Tate
Jordon Tate
Mrs. Pearline Tate
Adline Taylor
Mrs. Annie R. Taylor
J.D. Taylor
Mrs. Lillian K. Taylor
Mrs. Mary Taylor
Mrs. Sylvis Taylor
G.W. Temple Jr
Robert Thampson
Addrew E. Thomas
Mr. Charles Thomas
Mrs. Emma L. Thomas
Mrs. Frankie G. Thomas
Mr. John Thomas
Mrs. Lettie Thomas
Lizzie Thomas
Mrs. Lucy Thomas
Mandy Thomas
Sadie Thomas
Willie Thomas
Mrs. Wilma Thomas

Mrs. G.J. Thompkins
Mr. & Mrs. Joe Thompson
Mrs. Lillie Thompson
Mrs. Hattie Thorten
Mary Frances Thorton
Mrs. T.J. Todd
Thelma Todd
Dorothy Tolbert
Mrs. Irene Tolbert
Tom Tombleston
Virginia Tombleston
William Tompkins
Charlie Tone
Mrs. Mary Towns
Miss Ruby Towns
Samuel Towns
Miss Ella Louise Tripp
Miss Mary Tripp
Mrs. Beatrice Turk
Mrs. Inez Turner
Ethel Tyler
Henrietta Tyus
Mrs. B. Underwood
Matthew Underwood
Levi Charles Varner Jr
Miss Marion E. Vasser
Mrs. Shirley Vaughan
Mrs. Hazel Vincut
Miss Sarah Voltz
Willie Voltz
Bossie Walker
Charles A. Walker
Mrs. Clara Walker
Ella Walker
Fannie Walker

Mrs. H.O. Walker
Ivory James Walker
Mrs. Jennie Walker
Johnny M. Walker
L.C. Walker
Mrs. Maggie Walker
Margaret Walker
Miss Pearlie M. Walker
Mr. Petters Walker
Mr. Willie Walker Sr
T.L. Waller
Mrs. Dianna Walter
Mrs. Amanda Walton
Jesse Walton
I.E. Waltor
Francis Washington
Jeese Washington
John Washington
Miss Belzora Watters
Miss Corine Watters
Alex Watts
Mrs. Anna L. Watts
Arcene Watts
Mrs. Earl Watts
Mrs. Gertha Watts
Haywood Watts
Roosevelt Watts
Velma Watts
Arthur Webb
Johnson Webb Sr
Ocie Weeden
Mrs. Bertha Weeden
Mrs. Annie Welkins
Miss Frances Wells
Mrs. Mary Etta Wesley

Mrs. Alice West
Lozy West
Mr. Nathaniel West
Mr. John Westy
M.L. Wheeler
Mrs. Evelyn White
Mrs. Melvina White
Mrs. Mildred A. White
Nanie S. White
Ocie White
Annie William
Mrs. Annie M. William
Inola William
Reverend A. Williams
Abbie Williams
Anderson Williams
Andrew Williams
Ms Annuermell Williams
E.W. Williams
Eartha Williams
Mrs. Eddie Williams
Ella Mae Williams
Mrs. Ernestine Williams
George Williams
James Williams
Mrs. Laura Williams
Lawrence Williams
Mrs. M.E. Williams
Mrs. Martha Williams
Miss Nancy Williams

Mrs. Nettie E. Williams
Posey Williams
Mrs. R.H. Williams
Mrs. Rosa L. Williams
Teresa Williams
Mrs. Thelma Williams
Mrs. Hester Willis
Mrs. Lula Mae Willis
A.L. Wilson
Cora B. Wilson
Mrs. George E. Wilson
Jewel Janice Wilson
Mr. & Mrs. Winters
Alford Wood
Mrs. S.L. Woodrow
Mrs. L.A. Woodson
Mrs. Mildred F. Worford
Mrs. Lornie Wormley
M.J. Wormley
Robert Wormley
Mrs. Minnie L. Wyatt
Ruby Wynn
W.J. Yelder
Mrs. Elmira Young
Gilbert Young
Mrs. Julia Young
Marjorie Young
Melinda Young
W.W. Young

XII.

DON'T SELL OUT!

I often reflect on the time during the heat of the movement in 1965 when one of the members of Brown Chapel, Brother E.L. Moss, came to my office and said that a white man wanted to talk with me. I agreed to see him, but he wanted to take me downtown to his office. In the meantime, the mass meeting was in high gear. I got in his car and rode down to his office without the slightest idea what he wanted to talk to me about. His name was Mr. Coon, the bondsman for the city of Selma, Alabama.

We went into his office, sat down in a comfortable chair, and he began to explain what was on his mind.

"The Whites have always had a colored person in the colored community to serve as a liaison with the white community," he said. "We think you would make a good person for us." Then he placed in front of me a tablet with a dollar sign on it and said, "Write your figures on it."

"What would I have to do," I asked.

He said, "Keep us informed on what's going on in the community, close your church doors to the movement and we will take care of you!"

My answer was a resounding, "No! You are asking me to do something I have always fought against. I think I have about eight dollars in my pocket, but I am happy with that, because I got it honestly. You couldn't give me enough money to sell out my two boys, wife, and my race. You have the wrong man. Take me back to my church and my people where I belong."

That was more than thirty-seven years ago, but I have never regretted the firm stand I took then against the temptation to sell out the movement for a fifteen-cent lunch. A preacher must decide whether he is a prophet or a puppet. Reverend William Jones, in his book *Responsible Preaching*, asks us to take a serious look at the word "puppet." Look at its two syllables—the two words, pup and pet. Now, you know what a pup is; a pup is a canine with dog characteristics. A pup is not fully grown. A pet is something you play with (not to be taken seriously). A pup-pet. It suggests a leash and a handler. A pup-pet has no business standing in the pulpit, especially when the leash runs downtown to the powers that be. Puppets have human handlers, and the handlers dictate the puppet's movements.

I felt that the times were critical and called for a prophet to stand up. I was in a free pulpit and free church telling freedom's story in the name of *Him* that makes us free indeed. There is not enough power in City Hall or in the bondsman's office, nor is there enough gold in Fort Knox to cause me even to think about "selling out" on the issues of freedom and justice. Prophets don't hang out with politicians. Prophets don't eat the King's meat. Prophets don't appease for the sake of appointments. Prophets don't hang on to the apron strings for handouts. Prophets tell the truth about God. Prophets preach the word in season and out of season, in the pulpit and in the bondsman's office. The prophet puts God over government and Christ over culture.

Puppets court Caesar; prophets challenge Caesar. Puppets capitulate; prophets confront culture. The bondsman took me down to the briefing room, but he forgot that I have been in another room. It's a room higher than any room in the City of Selma, Alabama. It's the Upper Room. God established it. Jesus presides over it. The Holy Spirit fills it. That's my room. And in the Upper Room, I heard Jesus declare, *"Ye shall know the truth and the truth shall set you free." "Whatsoever a man soweth, that shall he also reap." "In the world ye shall have trials and tribulation, but be of good cheer I have overcome the world."*

I say again, I have never regretted not taking them up on their offer, because I put principal before cash and dignity before disgrace. I never wanted justice and equality just for me, but for everyone. For example, in Selma at one point they had a boycott on a garment factory. The meeting was held at a church near the factory. I went out to the meeting, and when I drove up to the church, I saw that the city had placed no parking signs all along the roadside. There was a police officer standing near the church. He walked up to my car and asked, "Where are you going Reverend Lewis? You are just out here to start trouble."

I said, "This is supposed to be a free country. Where can I park?"

He said, "Way down the road." That I did.

When I came back, he asked, "Where did you park?"

I said, "Way down the road."

He said, "I'm going to put a ticket on it." Of course he did!

The next day we had a meeting in the Mayor's office along with the Chief of Police. I mentioned to both of them about how the officer harassed me the day before and put a ticket on my car. The mayor and the Chief said, "Reverend Lewis, give the ticket to the chief and he will fix it for you."

I wanted to and asked, "But what about all the rest of the people who got tickets?"

They said, "Oh no."

I said, "If you can't fix theirs, then I don't want you just to fix mine! We must be concerned about the least of these."

Marchers at the peak of the Edmund Pettus Bridge, March 21, 1965. To Martin Luther King Jr.'s right is Ralph Abernathy, to his left RalphBurke. Reverend P. H. Lewis is behind Burke's left shoulder. Bodyguards march in the foreground.

XIII.

PROTEST AS A WEAPON AGAINST INJUSTICE

In 1787, Richard Allen devised the protest movement as a weapon against injustice. Behind this action by Allen was a feeling that as a man, although a Negro, he should be treated with dignity and respect, and should not suffer discrimination.

In 1955, Rosa Parks, as I said before, was a choir member of one of Allen's churches, the St. Paul A.M.E. Church in Montgomery, Alabama, and she refused to give up her seat to a white passenger, and this started the present-day Negro revolt. The revolt was not new but had its roots in a built-up feeling of resentment against discrimination and injustice over the years. Richard Allen lit the spark in 1787, and Rosa Parks was to light the spark again in 1955.

There was a certain duplicity in the attitude of this country, as it attempted to champion the cause of freedom throughout the world, and at the same time to deny it to Negroes within its own borders.

This is still true today, just as in the time of Richard Allen. America desired freedom from the British, but at the same time desired to hold Negroes in subjugation for life.

The radio and TV today, and other news media from time to time, blast forth the idea of democracy as a world concept, and naturally Negroes listen to these broad concepts and ideals, just as do other citizens in our country. A recent TV program told of one-third of a population going to bed hungry; and the next program told how some farmers received thousands of dollars for *not* planting certain crops.

Recent broadcasts told of the Apollo 12 leaving sixteen million dollars worth of equipment on the moon, plus an expense of three hundred sixty million dollars for the second moon voyage. In many cases, poverty and hunger could be eliminated by these funds. There seems to be a lack of priorities in our American system of values, and this situation more than anything else has caused the current Negro revolt. Negroes are beginning to see these misplaced values in our American commonwealth. We as a country find money for what we want to do, but fail to provide funds for things which need to be done. As a group, Negroes feel that they are still exploited, discriminated against, and mistreated in almost the same way today as in the day of Richard Allen. While all citizens of good will abhor violence, and believe that violence for Negroes is self-defeating, at the same time they abhor the system, which itself produces violence.

The Negro today lives for the most part in poverty, economic insecurity, and in ghetto districts, while the country flourishes in material wealth. We as a race are at the bottom of the ladder in economics, jobs, educational opportunities, political responsibilities, and national status.

The average Negro family is born into a trap of want and very limited opportunities, and only a very few escape therefrom. At any given time, statistics show that there are two-times as many jobless Negroes as whites, and even the major portion of those employed are in low-paying menial jobs.

The problem is compounded in this age of technology and automation. Discrimination, lack of education, and lack of training confine the race to the lowest rung of the ladder in employment, and every new technological development means that the Negro is the first to suffer from unemployment.

All these situations bring into focus injustices, which the race has endured for more than one hundred years since the Emancipation Proclamation, and in their own thinking, Blacks have decided that at any cost they are determined to break this unjust system. The Negro is willing to literally take the bull by the horns, because—as he says—his situation could not be any worse.

The direct protest first used by Richard Allen was found to be the best technique to throw the searchlight on injustices existing in our American way of life. How Allen seized upon this technique is one of the marvels of history. In slavery, there was very little discussion of ideas, and, except in a very few cases, slaves were prevented from learning to read and write. Families were torn apart, and even Allen's mother was sold away from other members of the immediate family. Yet, in some way, Allen seized upon the idea of peaceful protest as a means of righting social injustice. Protest seemed to disturb the peace and tranquillity of the entire community, and revealed in the spotlight of public opinion the existence of a cancer eating away at the fabric of our society. The peaceful protest is a powerful remedy to correct injustice, and by its very nature it throws the opposition into a state of utter confusion.

The peaceful protest seemingly attracts white friends to the cause of the Negro, and causes sympathy for him in his struggles. Perhaps one of the greatest demonstrations in history was the peaceful march on Washington in 1963 by more than two hundred fifty thousand people. A large percentage of these people were Whites who felt that Negroes should have their rights, and they were willing to sacrifice time and money in the fight.

This march had its origin in the mind of A. Philip Randolph, a member of an A.M.E. church, whose father was once pastor of the New Hope A.M.E. Church in Jacksonville, and the Chief Lieutenant for this march was Byard Ruskin, a graduate of Wilberforce University, a leading A.M.E. institution in Ohio.

Roy Wilkins, who threw the weight of the powerful N.A.A.C.P. behind this march, has strong A.M.E. connections. The march was perhaps the first organized operation among Negroes on a large scale, and was accorded the respect and coverage from the national press and news media which it deserved. The march was almost universally endorsed by all denominations in America, and the A.M.E. Church threw the full weight of its organization in support of this confrontation.

The world, by means of the TV news media, had an opportunity to view the Negro in the serious business of trying to throw oppression off his back. The fact that the demonstration was peaceful in every respect shocked the world, as many prophets anticipated violence and bloodshed. The world listened to intelligent Negroes explain how, as a race and as a people who had given all to America, they have nonetheless been exploited and mistreated—they now had decided that patience, docility, submissiveness, and begging were no longer virtues. It is time now, said many Negroes, to throw the weight of oppression off our backs, regardless of consequences.

If anyone expected to see the joking, funny, stereotyped, and easy-going Negro, they were sadly disappointed. They saw, rather, a determined newer breed of Negro, using the technique of peaceful protest devised by Richard Allen in 1787. What worked in 1787 succeeded in 1963. From the pamphlet "Allen and Present-day Social Problems" by Howard D. Gregg, I quote the following:

"The progress of the Negro in civil, political, economic, and educational spheres today is due perhaps more to organized efforts on the part of Negroes themselves than to any other force. It is true that liberalism has had a day in court and that international pressures have been in evidence, but the main lever that has turned the fulcrum for human progress for the Negro has been the Negro himself. It may also be said that their efforts achieved results only when they were helped by the White House. In fact, the dynamo behind their liberal efforts, to an extent, has been agitation and protests on the part of organized Negro groups.

"Seventy-seven years before the Emancipation Proclamation, Richard Allen reasoned that what one alone could not do, several banded together in united effort could achieve. The fact that the first organizational protest efforts among Negroes centered in the church is as it should be. The fact that the early efforts of Allen to perfect an organization met opposition does not appear strange among our people.

"In organizing a group of Negroes to leave St. George's Church as a protest because of unfair treatment due to race, Richard Allen was indirectly establishing a technique of procedure for minority groups and at the same time laid the foundation for the great African Methodist Episcopal Church. It was conceded many years later during the period of protests over slavery that however eloquent the appeal of white men may be on behalf of the slave, the Negro plead-ing his own case could wield more effective blows against the system.

"Leadership qualities demonstrated by Richard Allen were seemingly magnetic and compelling. Organizations are usually formed around great personalities, and this first organizational protest movement was an exception to this general rule. As Allen walked out of St. George's Church, others followed. One, Jane Ann Murky, an unsung hero, left St. George's Church along with others, and although they did not gain renown, they represented the early vanguard who got African Methodism going in it's early stages. The leadership qualities of Allen were also shown when subsequent developments caused many to draw away in the face of opposition. Allen indeed was a born leader, and even as a slave these characteristics were very evident."

The Negro at the time of Richard Allen was in need of just such a personality as his—one who could formulate into structural organization the basic ideals of the race. Remember that Negroes were simply tolerated and had no particular status that would guarantee respectability. There were no innate rights which Whites were compelled to respect, and no agitation for dignity had ever been made before in America on the part of Negroes. This act, therefore, on the part of Negroes as they walked out of St. George's Church in Philadelphia because of unfair treatment, had widespread repercussions among Negroes. It probably caused a feeling of somebodyness to permeate the race for the first time in history. Remember that slave life did everything possible to take away from the Negro the feeling that he was somebody. As I said earlier, families were torn apart—sold at will. Mothers were sold away from children, and brothers and sisters were also sold separately. Even religious leaders made much of that passage of scripture, which advised servants to obey their masters. Powerful sermons were preached using this text as a background. The institution of slavery was deeply entrenched in the economy of America. Men were known by the position they took on this important question, and political futures were dependent upon their vigorous interpretation of the Negro as a predestined "hewer of wood and drawer of water." For a Negro, therefore, to object to unfair treatment at the hands of Whites was probably as significant as the incident itself.

The fact that Allen and his little band of followers desired dignity and respect must have shocked the sensibilities of the entire area. Perhaps it took days, maybe weeks, for the idea to sink in. Remember that Richard Allen was no troublemaker and evidently was willing to compromise. The very fact that he went to the gallery shows a desire to bend over backwards, apparently to avoid disrupting the religious service.

Richard Allen deserves credit not only for the basic organizational structure of the African Methodist Episcopal Church but for his influence upon the united actions of Negroes for their own welfare and progress. The movement started by him evidently met at intervals, since Carter G. Woodson refers to organized efforts among Negroes fourteen years later in 1930, just prior to the death of Richard Allen. The question of colonization of Negroes evidently was not dead. In reply to the suggestion that the Negro emigrate under the protection of the American Colonization Society, a few bold thinkers like Peter Williams, Peter Volgelsang, Thomas L. Jennings, and Richard Allen proposed a convention of the leaders of the Negroes in the United States. A preliminary meeting was held in Philadelphia on September 15, 1830. Delegates from seven states were present. Richard Allen was made president; Dr. Belfast Burton of Philadelphia and Austin Steward of Rochester, vice-presidents; Junius C. Morrell of Philadelphia secretary; and Robert Cowley from Maryland assistant secretary. At the time of this meeting, Allen was near the end of his career. He died several months later, but his success in starting organized efforts by Negroes continues even to this day.

After Allen's death in 1830 it appears that Negroes tended to meet in annual conventions. They met not only in Philadelphia,

110

but also in other cities. These meetings were held almost regularly until the Civil War, and the part played by Richard Allen in crystallizing sentiment in these meetings for the emancipation to come some thirty-three years after his death may never be known. The gatherings were usually addressed by the most prominent Negroes of the day, and by sympathetic and liberal Whites. One of these conventions sent out addresses to Negroes both free and enslaved encouraging them to "struggle upward" and also to conduct themselves so as to win friends for their cause throughout the world. Memorials praying for the abolition of slavery and the improvement of the free people of color were usually sent to the state legislatures and to Congress. Eight states were officially represented at the meeting in 1832—with thirty authentic representatives. Fifty-eight delegates were present a year later. The growth of vital issues caused the number of delegates to increase, and with the discussion over the expansion of slave territory and the Dred Scot Decision, the meetings could never die.

The acuteness of the Negro problem crystallized Negro group thinking, and varied suggestions were made for a solution. The free Negro was a menace to slavery and, hence, was driven out of the south. This presented embarrassment to poor Whites in the North where they fled. Some northern counties advocated denying admission to free Negroes. The plight of the free Negro was indeed pitiful. As Dr. Howard Gregg said, *"They were discriminated against by employers who preferred Whites. They were denied consideration in the courts when they appealed to them, and truly the Negro was indeed between the devil and the deep sea. They were subjected to attacks by mobs spurred on to action by almost any petty offense committed by one of the free population of color."*

While Richard Allen passed on to his reward in 1830, the spirit of united actions started by him was very necessary to

111

Negroes who had problems to solve and issues to meet. These problems were numerous. Negroes not only faced difficulties in labor and competition with poor Whites, but they were disfranchised. To sum up, in colonial times, the free Negro was excluded from the suffrage not only in Georgia, South Carolina, and Virginia, but in the border states. Delaware disfranchised the Negro in 1792, Maryland in 1783 and 1810. In the Southeast, Florida disfranchised Negroes in 1845, and in the Southwest, Louisiana disfranchised them in 1812, Mississippi in 1817, Alabama in 1819, Missouri in 1821, Arkansas in 1836, Texas in 1845, and Georgia, in her constitution of 1777, confined voting to white males; but this was omitted in the constitution of 1789 and 1798.

As slavery grew to a system and the cotton kingdom began to expand into imperial White domination, a free Negro was a contradiction, a threat, and a menace. As a thief and a vagabond he threatened society, but as an educated property holder, a successful mechanic, or even professional man, he more than threatened slavery. He contradicted and undermined it. He must therefore be surpressed, enslaved; colonized. And nothing so bad could be said about him that did not easily appear as true to slave holders. Allen, in starting protest movements in his day, was lighting a fuse, which was destined to start a flame, which would finally burn the shackles of slavery asunder. Slavery, which was embedded deeply not only in the social structure of the South but also in the northern manufacturing system, cheapened the state and respectability of free Negroes and embarrassed them in their protests for equality of opportunity.

It should be realized that any protest movement designed to bring about dignity and respect will have wholesome effects upon the protesting people. It brings them together as a unified group and causes them to rethink their position and status in society. An organized protest movement against injustice not only is wholesome for the members themselves but also invites sympathy and help from others. How many friends the protest movement started by Allen won for the cause of the enslaved Negro may never be known, but it is reasonably certain that many joined in these efforts, and Allen years later must have smiled from above when he saw the forces of righteousness overcome the forces of evil. In the structure of modern society today, as in the days of Allen, very little can be accomplished through an individual. One alone is almost powerless to attack the entrenched evil. It is like butting one's head against the proverbial brick wall. It is singular that Richard Allen, although a man without previous experience, used the system of organized protest as a means of making social wrongs right. The technique he devised is still the most powerful weapon for minority groups, and even to this day, it is deemed to be the most effective method of protest in America. While subsequent protest movements have followed various forms, we will always look back to the origin of organized protest on the part of Negroes realizing that the entire Negro race owes a debt of gratitude to Richard Allen, the forerunner of organized protest movements among Negroes.

XIV.

THE SHARE CROPPER

In 1968, the members of the Trustee Board of Daniel Payne College received a letter from Hayes Aircraft, located under the hill adjacent to our property, asking us to move from 6415 Washington Boulevard, Birmingham, Alabama, to another location. We agreed to accept the offer of five hundred thousand dollars for twenty acres of land and started looking for another site. At that time I was pastoring at Brown Chapel A.M.E. in Selma. I talked to city officials there about the possibility of moving the school back to Selma.

They went for the idea, stating what a great thing it would be to have a senior college in the area to feed off of the many junior colleges in the city and in surrounding counties. I called my Bishop and asked him to come to Selma. I set up a meeting with the mayor, probate judge, architect, and members of the city council. It was a very positive meeting—the red carpet was rolled out for the school. The location was selected and we discussed lights, streets, water, curbs, gutters—the works.

But when white folks started talking about the "Black Belt" area, my Bishop's countenance changed, and he soon closed the

114

meeting. I didn't know why until later on when I asked him what he thought of the meeting. He said, to my surprise, "I didn't like to hear white folks calling colored folks black."

I said to him, "Bishop you're wrong, they were not talking about people. They were referring to the rich black soil."

The "Black Belt" consisted of soil that can produce corn, peanuts, cotton, peas, sweet potatoes—you name it. But you also find black people who rented from "Mr. Charlie," the plantation owner. Some who leased land were never able to get out of debt. The farmer had to be advanced money to plant his crop and then get money to gather his crop. The Negro and his family would work like "minute men" all year growing the crop. When setting-up time came, after making thirty bails of cotton, the landlord would tell him, "Boy, if you would have made two more bails, you would be out of debt." This poor black man would go back to work another year, work even harder and make thirty-three bails of cotton, but when setting-up time came, Mr. Charlie would tell him again, "If you had made five more bails, you would sure enough get out of debt." This was the kind of endless cycle that went on for years.

In the 1950's, when the word got around that beef was going to be the "in thing" in the future, many of the sharecroppers were told that, "If your wife can't have a white-faced calf next year, you will have to move from my place. In many instances, this was a blessing in disguise for the sharecroppers. For in point of fact, often they had raised enough cotton to have paid for not just the rent and seeds, but to have bought the plantations. There is more than one way to rob a man. You can rob him with a gun. You can rob him with a knife, and you can rob a man or woman with a pencil or an ink pen.

Sharecroppers would also lease land from the plantation owner. For example, they would lease a hundred acres of land from Mr. Charlie. The tenant would then let forty of the hundred acres lay up, knowing that the federal government would pay him for not planting cotton on that forty acres. When he would get the check from the government, the landlord would demand the tennant give him the check, because, he said, he owned the land.

In the 1960's, this kind of deal was reported to the federal government, and the government made the landlords pay back all the money to the rightful owners. Thank God for the federal government. Where would black folks be if it was not for the Lord and the federal government?

At one point in America, it has been alleged that black folks owned more than sixteen millions acres of land. Today that figure may be less than eight million acres. Much of it was lost by squatter's rights, meaning that if someone runs you off of your land and you stay off of it for a certain number of years, and they pay the taxes on it, the tax payer would own the land. Many of these kinds of things happened to black folks in the south. This is called confiscation and stealing.

The other method was manipulation. I had a cousin whose daddy died in 1953, leaving the four children more than four hundred acres of land paid for—only the tax had to be paid on it each year. In 1957, the son worked at a saw mill; he went to his boss and asked him to finance a 1954 Chevrolet car that cost about three thousand dollars. The boss gave him the money to purchase the car, but had him sign some papers that said a whole lot that the man didn't understand. Things like, "Go on and drive the car and I will tell you when you need to pay me." This he did. He drove the car for years. Then one day the man called him into the office and asked him, "When are you going to pay on your car?" The man asked how much he owed. Then the man pulled out papers that he had signed, which read that, failing to meet the payments, the full amount was due—or the boss could cut enough timber off the land to pay the debt owed. They cut timber, but could not cut enough timber to satisfy the man. He ended up losing the four hundred acres over a three thousand dollar car.

What a shame! What a price to pay. These and other means were used to cheat black folks out of their land.

Getting Ready To Plant Cotton

First you have to get the ground ready by clearing the land of bushes. Then you get the mule or horse and the plow and you broadcast the area you are going to use. You then lay out your rows with what is known as a scooter, and put down your fertilizer with what is known as a fertilizer distributor—or you can spread it with your hands. After this you get what is known as a turnplow, fasten it to the metal foot of the plow, then you cover up the fertilizer by building a bed. After a bed is completed, you get the scooter again and open up the bed about one or two inches. Then you get a cotton planter and you plant the cotton seeds. After the cotton comes up about two or three inches tall, you get the turnplow again, and barrow off the cotton; then you get what is known as a hoe and you chop the cotton by pulling grass out of the cotton and the dirt away from the cotton. After you finish chopping the cotton, then you get what is known as a solid suite to dirt the cotton by putting dirt up around the cotton; Getting the turnplow yet again, you bust the middle out by throwing dirt toward the cotton.

After a few weeks you take the turnplow and barrow the cotton off again. Now it's time to hoe the cotton. This time you get grass out and you pull the dirt around the cotton. Then you get the solid suite and you dirt the cotton again. After dirting, you get what is known as a buzzer wing suite and burst the middle out by throwing dirt right and left.

After the cotton is tall enough and it starts blooming, it's time to start poisoning the cotton to keep the boll weeviles from eating it up. The boll weeviles can really do a job on cotton. In a county in South Alabama, the boll weeviles ate up all the cotton, and it was too late in the year to plant over. So they planted peanuts instead. Through their bad experience they discovered that the land was better for peanuts, so from then on they planted peanuts. That place is called the "Peanut Session of the South."

To plow the cotton for the last time is called "layby." In this part of the county where the boll weeviles ate up the cotton, they had to plow it up because it was too late to replant it. They were so proud of what the boll weeviles did that they had a giant-size boll weevile made and mounted it in the town square of Enterprise, Alabama.

After layby (which means it's the last time to plow the cotton for the year), you must continue to poison the cotton for boll weeviles until the bolls on the cotton began to open. After the bolls are fully opened and the cotton begins to hang out of the bolls, it's time to pick cotton. To pick the cotton, you get a sack, tie a wide strap on the sack and put it on your shoulder, and you pull the cotton from the bolls and place the cotton in the sack. It takes about fourteen or fifteen hundred pounds to make a bail of cotton.

After the cotton is picked, you load it on the two-horse wagon with a bail body and you haul it to the gin house to be ginned, and you sell it for the going price. The farmer usually gets up early in the morning, around five o'clock. He has to feed the chickens, slop the hogs, feed the mules or horses or cows, and then himself. A farmer usually eats three meals a day:

breakfast, dinner and supper. He and his family go to bed around eight or nine o'clock at night. Most farmers plant what they eat, and most definitely eat what they plant and grow.

On many farms, you will see cattle and milk cows. The farmer lets the milk cows graze all day, and late in the afternoon, he gets the milk cows from the pasture and puts them in a "cow pen" and milks them by squeezing milk from the udder of the cow. Usually you can get one, two, or three gallons of milk from each cow, depending on the breed of cow you are milking.

The milk is strained, then put in a churn and allowed to set for half a day or so until it clabbers. With a dask—that is, a stick about an inch in diameter with a bottom that looks like a cross—the farmer churns the milk by lifting the dask up and down for about fifteen or twenty minutes, until the butter comes. He and his family will use the butter to make pound cakes, and with syrup on biscuits, grits, rice, corn bread, et cetera.

Just before hog-killing time, the farmer will sort out the hogs he wants to kill. First, he puts them up off the ground in a special pen so that the hogs won't have much moving room. Then he'll feed them special food. This is called "fattening up to kill." When he feels that they are fat enough, he picks the coldest day of winter to kill hogs. He gets some water and puts it in a big pot and heats the water until it boils. He puts the water in a big barrel. To kill the hog, he hits it on the head with an ax, then stabs it in the heart to bleed the animal. After the bleeding, he places it in the hot water to get the hair off by scraping. The hot water makes it easy to come off.

When all the hair is off, he hangs the hog up and washes it off really well. Then he guts the hog by taking out the intestines, the liver, lungs, heart, kidneys, and chitterlings, et cetera. He washes the liver, lungs, and the chitterlings, et cetera. Now, after washing the inside of the hog thoroughly, it's time to cut the hog up in various parts, such as hams, pork chops, ribs, pig's feet, sausage, and chitterlings, et cetera. The farmer preserves his meat by salting it down and putting it in a barrel where it can be kept indefinitely.

XV

THE BLACK CODES

Louisiana, 1865

1. An Act To Provide for and Regulate Labor Contracts for Agricultural Pursuits.[1]

Section 1. Be it enacted by the Senate and House of Representatives of the State of Louisiana in general assembly convened, That all persons employed as laborers in agricultural pursuits shall be required, during the first ten days of the month of January of each year, to make contracts for labor for the then ensuing year, or for the year next ensuing the termination of their present contracts. All contracts for labor for agricultural purposes shall be made in writing, signed by the employer, and shall be made in the presence of a Justice of Peace and two disinterested witnesses, in whose presence the contract shall be

---

[1] Acts of the General Assembly of Louisiana Regulating Labor, Extra Session, 1865, p. 3ff. Reprinted in Henry Steele Commager, *Documents of American History* (New York: Appleton-Century-Crofts, Inc., 1958), p. 455.

read to the laborer, and when assented to and signed by latter, shall be considered as binding for the time prescribed. . . .

Section 2. Every laborer shall have full and perfect liberty to choose his employer, but, when once chosen, he shall not be allowed to leave his place of employment until the fulfillment of his contract . . .and if they do so leave, without cause or permission, they shall forfeit all wages earned to the time of abandonment. . . .

Section 7. All employers failing to comply with their contracts shall, upon conviction, be fined an amount double that due the laborer. . . to be paid to the laborer; and any inhumanity, cruelty, or neglect of duty on the part of the employer shall be summarily punished by fines . . .to be paid to the injured party. . . .

Section 8. Be it further enacted, &c., That in case of sickness of the laborer, wages for the time lost shall be deducted, and also on where sickness is feigned for purposes of idleness, and also on refusal to work according to contract, double the amount of wages shall be deducted for the time lost; and also where rations have been furnished; and should the refusal to work continue beyond three days, the offender shall be reported to a Justice of Peace, and shall be forced to labor on roads, levees, and other public works, without pay, until the offender consents to return to his labor.

Section 9. Be it further enacted, &c., That, when in health, the laborer shall work ten hours during the day in summer, and nine hours during the day in winter, unless otherwise stipulated in the labor contract; he shall obey all proper orders of his employer or agent; take proper care of his work mules, horses, oxen, stock; also of all agricultural implements; and employers shall have the right to make a reasonable deduction from the laborer's wages for injuries done to animals or agricultural implements committed to his care, or for bad negligent work. Bad work shall not be allowed. Failing to obey reasonable orders, neglect of duty, and leaving home without permission will be deemed disobedience; imprudence, swearing, or indecent language to or in the presence of the employer, his family, or agent, or quarreling and fighting with one another, shall be deemed disobedience. For any disobedience a fine of one dollar shall be imposed on and paid by the offender. For all lost time from work-hours, unless in case of sickness, the laborer shall be fined twenty-five cents per hour. For all absence from home without leave he will be fined two dollars per day. Laborer will not be required to labor on the Sabbath unless by special contract. For all thefts of the laborer from the employer of agricultural products, hogs, sheep, poultry, or any other property of employer, willful destruction of property or injury, the laborer shall pay the employer double the amount of the value of the property stolen, destroyed, or injured, one-half to be paid to the employed and the other half to be placed in the general fund provided in this section. No live stock shall be allowed to laborer without permission of the employer. Laborers shall not receive visitors during work-hours. All difficulties arising between employers and laborers under this section, shall be settled by the former; if not satisfactory to the laborers, an appeal may be had to the nearest Justice of Peace and two freeholders, citizens, one of said citizens to be selected by the employer and the other by the laborer; and all fines imposed and collected under this section shall be deducted from wages due, and shall be placed in a common fund, to be divided among the other laborers on the plantation, except as provided for above. . . .

Section 10. Be it further enacted, &c., That for gross misconduct on the part of the laborer, such as insubordination, habitual laziness, frequent acts of violation of his contract or the laws of the State, he may be dismissed by his employer; nevertheless, the laborer shall have the right to resist his dismissal and to a redress of his wrongs by an appeal to a Justice of the Peace and freeholders, citizens of the parish, one of the freeholders to be selected by himself and the other by his employer.

2. **An Act Relative to Apprentices and Indentured Servants**

Section 1. Be it enacted. . . That it shall be the duty of Sheriffs, Justice of Peace, and other Civil officers of this State, to report. . . for each and every year, all persons under the age of eighteen years, if female, and twenty-one, if males, who are orphans, or whose parents. . . have not the means, or who refuse to provide for and maintain said minors; and thereupon it shall be the duty of the Clerk of the District Courts. . . to examine whether the party or parties so reported from time to time, come within the purview and meaning of this Act, and if so, to apprentice said minor or minors, in manner and form as prescribed by the Civil Code. . . .

Section 2. That persons, who have attained the age of majority. . . may bind themselves to services to be performed in this State, for the term of five years, on such terms as they may stipulate, as domestic servants, and to work on farms, plantations, or in manufacturing establishments, which contracts shall be valid and binding on the parties to the same.

Section 3. That in all cases where the age of the minor can not be ascertained by record testimony, the Clerk of the District Courts, Mayor and President of the Police Jury, or Justice of the Peace aforesaid, shall fix the age, according to the best evidence before them. . . .

Mississippi, 1865[2]

1. Civil Rights of Freedmen in Mississippi

Section 1. Be it enacted. . . . That all freedmen, free negroes, and mulattoes may sue and be sued, implead and be impleaded in all the courts of law and equity of this State, and may acquire personal property, and chooses in action, by descent or purchase, and may dispose of the same in the same manner and to the same extent that white persons may: Provided, That the provisions of this section shall not be so construed as to allow any freedman, free negro, or mulatto to rent or lease any lands or tenements except in incorporated cities or towns, in which places the corporate authorities shall control the same. . . .

Section 3. . . .All freedmen, free negroes, or mulattoes who do now and have herebefore lived and cohabited together as husband and wife shall be taken and held in law as legally married, and the issue shall be taken and held as legitimate for all purposes; that it shall not be lawful for any freedman, free negro, or mulatto to intermarry with any white person; nor for any white to intermarry with any freedman, free negro, or mulatto; and any person who shall so intermarry, shall be deemed guilty of a felony, and on conviction thereof shall be confined in the State penitentiary for life; and those shall be deemed freedmen, free negroes, and mulattoes who are of pure negro blood, and

---

2 Laws of Mississippi, 1865, p. 82ff, reprinted in ibid., p. 452.

those descended from a negro to the third generation, inclusive, though one ancestor in each generation may have been a white person. . . .

Section 6. . . .All contracts for labor made with freedmen, free negroes, and mulattoes for a longer period than one month shall be in writing, and in duplicate, attested and read to said freedman, free negro, mulatto by a beat, city or county officer, or two disinterested white persons of the county in which the labor is to be performed, of which each party shall have one; and said contracts shall be taken and held as entire contracts, and if the laborer shall quit the service of employer before the expiration of his term of service, without good cause, he shall forfeit his wages for that year up to the time of quitting.

Section 7. . . .Every civil officer shall, and every person may, arrest and carry back to his or her legal employer any freedman, free negro, or mulatto who shall have quit the service of his employer before the expiration of his or her term of service without good cause; and said officer and said person shall be entitled to receive for arresting and carrying back every deserting employee aforesaid the sum of five dollars, and ten cents per mile from the place of arrest to the place of delivery; and the same shall be paid by the employer, and held as a set-off for so much against the wages of said employee: Provided, that said arrested party, after being so returned, may appeal to the Justice of the Peace or member of the board of police of the county, who, on notice to the alleged employer, shall try summarily whether said appellant is legally employed by alleged employer, and has good cause to quit said employer. . . .

2. Mississippi Apprentice Law

Section 1. . . . .It shall be the duty of all sheriffs, Justice of the Peace, and other civil officers of the several counties of this State, to report to the probate courts of their respective counties semi-annually, at the January and July terms of said courts, all freedmen, free negroes, and mulattoes, under the age of eighteen, in their respective counties, beats or districts, who are orphans, or whose parent or parents have not the means or who refuse to provide for and support each minor; and thereupon it shall be the duty of said probate court to order the clerk of said court to apprentice said minor to some competent and suitable person, on such terms as the court may direct, having a particular care to the interest of said minor: Provided, that the former owner of said minors shall have the preference when, in the opinion of the court, he or she shall be a suitable person for that purpose.

Section 2. . . . .The said court shall be fully satisfied that the person or persons to whom said minor shall be apprenticed shall be a suitable person to have the charge and care of said minor, and fully to protect the interest of said minor. The said court shall require the said master or mistress to execute bond and security, payable to the State of Mississippi, conditioned that he or she shall furnish said minor with sufficient food and clothing; to treat said minor humanely; furnish medical attention in case of sickness; teach, or cause to be taught, him or her to read and write, if under fifteen years old, and will conform to any law that may be hereafter passed for the regulation of the duties and relation of master and apprentice. . . .

Section 3. . . .In the management and control of said apprentice, said master or mistress shall have the power to inflict such moderate corporal chastisement as a father or guardian is allowed to inflict on his or her child or ward at common law: Provided, that in no case shall cruel or inhuman punishment be inflicted.

Section 4. . . .If any apprentice shall leave the employment of his or her master or mistress, without his or her consent, said master or mistress may pursue and recapture said apprentice, and bring him or her before any justice of the peace of the county, whose duty it shall be to remand said apprentice to the service of his or her master or mistress; and in the event of a refusal on the part of said apprentice so to return, then said justice shall commit said apprentice to the jail of said county, on failure to give bond, to the next term of the county court; and it shall be the duty of said court at the first term thereafter to investigate said case, and if the court shall be of opinion that said apprentice left the employment of his or her master or mistress without good cause, to order him or her to be punished, as provided for the punishment of hired freedmen, as may be from time to time provided for by law for desertion, until he or she shall agree to return to the service of his or her master or mistress: . . .if the court shall believe that said apprentice had good cause to quit from said indenture, and also enter a judgment against the master or mistress for not more than one hundred dollars, for use and benefit of said apprentice. . . .

3.   Mississippi Vagrant Law

Section 1. Be it enacted, etc., . . .That all rogues and vagabonds, idle and dissipated persons, beggars, jugglers, or persons practicing unlawful games or plays, runaways, common drunkards, common night-walkers, pilferers, lewd, wanton, or lascivious persons, in speech or behavior, common railers and brawlers, persons who neglect their calling or employment, misspend what they earn, or do not provide for the support of themselves or their families, or dependents, and all other idle and disorderly persons, including all who neglect all lawful business, habitually misspend their time by frequenting houses of ill-fame, gaming-housing, or tippling shops, shall be deemed and considered vagrants, under the provisions of this act, and upon conviction thereof shall be fined not exceeding one hundred dollars, with all accruing costs, and be imprisoned at the discretion of the court, not exceeding ten days.

Section 2. . . .All freedmen, free negroes and mulattoes in this State, over the age of eighteen years, found on the second Monday in January, 1866, or thereafter, with no lawful employment or business, or found unlawfully assembling themselves together, either in the day or night time, and all white persons so assembling themselves with freedmen, free negroes, or mulattoes, or usually associating with freedmen, free negroes, or mulattoes, on terms of equality, or living in adultery or fornication with a freed woman, a free negro or mulatto, shall be deemed vagrants, and on conviction thereof shall be fined in a sum not exceeding, in the case of a freedman, free negro or mulatto, fifty dollars, and a white man two hundred dollars, and imprisoned at the discretion of the court, the free negro not exceeding ten days, and the white man not exceeding six months. . . .

4. Penal Laws of Mississippi

Section 1. Be it enacted. . . That no freedman, free negro or mulatto, not in the military service of the United States government, and not licensed so to do by the board of police of his or her county, shall keep or carry firearms of any kind, or any ammunition, dirk or Bowie knife, and on conviction thereof in the county court shall be punished by fine, not exceeding ten dollars, and pay costs of such proceedings, and all such arms or ammunition shall be forfeited to the informer; and it shall be the duty of every civil and military officer to arrest any freedman, free negro, or mulatto found with any such arms or ammunition, and cause him or her to be committed to trial in default of bail.

Section 2. Any freedman, free negro, or mulatto committing riots, routs, affrays, trespasses, malicious mischief, cruel treatment to animals, seditious speeches, insulting gestures, language, or acts, or assaults on any person, disturbance of the peace, exercising the function of a minister of the Gospel without a license from some regularly organized church, vending spirituous or intoxicating liquors, or committing any other misdemeanor, the punishment of which is not specifically provided for by law, shall, upon conviction thereof in the county court, be fined not less than ten dollars, and not more than one hundred dollars, and may be imprisoned at the discretion of the court, not exceeding thirty days. . . .

Section 5. If any freedman, free negro, or mulatto, convicted of any of the misdemeanors provided against in this act, shall fail or refuse for the space of five days, after conviction, to pay the fine and costs imposed, such person shall be hired out by the sheriff or other officer, at public outery, to any white person who will pay said fine and all costs, and take said convict for the shortest time.

XVI.

PETITION TO CONGRESS AGAINST VIOLENCE[3]

To The Senate and House of Representatives in Congress assembled: We the Colored Citizens of Frankfort and vicinity do this day memorialize your honorable bodies upon the condition of affairs now existing in this the state of Kentucky. We would respectfully state that life, liberty and property are unprotected among the colored race of this state. Organized bands of desperate and lawless men mainly composed of soldiers of the late rebel Armies, armed, disciplined and disguised and bound by Oath and secret obligations, have by force, terror, and violence subverted all civil society among colored people, thus utterly rendering insecure the safety of persons and property, overthrowing all those rights which are the primary basis and objects of the Government, which are expressly guaranteed to us by the Constitution of the United States as amended; We believe you are not familiar with the description of the Ku Klux

---

[3]   U. S. Senate, 42d Congress, 1st Session.

Klans riding nightly over the country, going from County to County and in the County towns spreading terror wherever they go, by robbing, whipping, ravishing, and killing our people without provocation, compelling colored people to brake the ice and bathe in the chilly waters of the Kentucky River.

The Legislation has adjourned they refuse to enact any laws to suppress Ku Klux disorder. We regard them as now being licensed to continue their dark and bloody deeds under cover of the dark night. They refuse to allow us to testify in the state courts where a white man is concerned. We find their deeds are perpetrated only upon colored men and white Republicans. We also find that for our services to the Government and our race we have become the special object of hatred and persecution at the hands of the Democratic party. Our people are driven from their homes in great numbers having no redress only in the United States Courts, which is in many cases unable to reach them. We would state that we have been law-abiding citizens, pay out tax and in many parts of the state our people have been driven from the poles [sic], refused the right to vote. Many have been slaughtered while attempting to vote, we ask how long is this state of things to last.

We appeal to you as law-abiding citizens to enact some laws that will protect us. And that will enable us to exercise the rights of citizens. We see that the senator from this state denies there being organized Bands of desperadoes in the state, for information we lay before you a number of violent acts occurred during his Administration. Although he Stevenson[4] says a half dozen instances of violence did occur these are not more than one half the acts that have occurred. The Democratic party has here a political organization composed only of

4 Governor—later, Senator—John W. Stevenson.

Democrats, not a single Republican can join them where many of these acts have been committed, it has been proven that they were the men, don with Armies from the State Arsenal. We pray you will take steps to remedy these evils.

March 25, 1871

Henry Marrs, Teacher colored school
Henry Lynn, Livery stable keeper
N. N. Trumbo, Grocer
Samuel Damsey, B. Smith [Blacksmith]
B. T. Crampton, Barber
Committee

1. A mob visited Harrodsburg in Mercer County to take from jail a man named Robertson, November 14, 1867.

2. Smith—attacked and whipped by regulation in Zelun County, November, 1867.

3. Colored schoolhouse burned by incendiaries in Breckinridge, December 24, 1867.

4. A Negro, Jim Macklin, was taken from jail in Frankfort and hung by a mob, January 28, 1868.

5. Sam Davis—hung by mob in Harrodsburg, May 28, 1868.

6. William Pierce—hung by a mob in Christian, July 12, 1868.

7. George Roger—hung by a mob in Bradsfordville, Martin County, July 11, 1868.

8. Colored School Exhibition at Midway, attacked by a mob, July 31, 1868.

9. Seven people ordered to leave their homes at Sandford, Kentucky, August 7, 1868.

10. Silas Woodford, age sixty—badly beaten by disguised mob. Mary Smith Curtis and Margaret Mosby were also badly beaten near Keene, Jessemine County, August, 1868.

11. Cabe Fields—shot and killed by disguised men near Keene, Jessemine County, August 3, 1868.

12. James Gaines—expelled from Anderson by Ku Klux Klan, August, 1868.

13. James Parker—killed by Ku Klux Klan, Pulaski, August, 1868.

14. Noah Blankenship—whipped by a mob in Pulaski County, August, 1868.

15. Negroes attacked, robbed, and driven from Summerville in Green County, August 21, 1868.

16. William Gibson and John Gibson—hung by a mob in Washington County, August, 1868.

17. F.H. Montford—hung by a mob near Cogers landing in Jessemine County, August 28, 1868.

18. William Glassgow—killed by a mob in Warren County, September 5, 1868.

19. Negro hung by a mob, September, 1868.

20. Two Negroes beaten by Ku Klux Klan in Anderson County, September 11, 1868.

21. Mob attacked house of Oliver Stone in Fayette County, September 11, 1868.

22. Mob attacked Cumins house in Pulaski County. Cumins, his daughter, and a man named Adams were killed in the attack, September 18, 1868.

23. U.S. Marshall Meriwether—attacked, captured, and beaten to death in Larue County by a mob, September, 1868.

24. Richardson house attacked in Conishville by a mob and Crasban was killed, September 28, 1868.

25. Mob attacked Negro cabin at Hanging Forks in Lincoln County. John Mosteran was killed, and Cash and Coffey were killed, September, 1869.

26. Terry Laws and James Ryan—hung by a mob in Nicholasville, October 26, 1868.

27. Attack on Negro cabin in Spencer County—a woman outraged, December, 1868.

28. Two Negroes were shot by Ku Klux Klan at Sulphur Springs in Union County, December, 1868.

29. Negro shot at Morganfield, Union County, December, 1868.

30. Mob visited Erwin Burris' house of Jesse Davis in Lincoln County, January, 1869.

31. William Parker—whipped by Ku Klux Klan in Lincoln County, January 20, 1869.

32. Mob attacked and fired into house of Jesse Davises in Lincoln County, January 20, 1869.

135

33. Spears taken from his room at Harrodsburg by disguised men, January 19, 1869.

34. Albert Bradford—killed by disguised men in Scott County, January 20, 1869.

35. Ku Klux Klan whipped boy at Standford, March 12, 1869.

36. Mob attacked Frank Bournes' house in Jessemine County. Roberts was killed in March, 1869.

37. Geo Bratcher—hung by a mob on Sugar Creek in Garrard County, March 30, 1869.

38. John Penny—hung by a mob at Nevada, Mercer County, May 29, 1869.

39. Ku Klux Klan whipped Lucien Green in Lincoln County, June, 1869.

40. Miller—whipped by Ku Klux Klan in Madison County, July 2, 1869.

41. Chas Hendenson—shot and his wife was killed by a mob at Silver Creek, Madison County, July, 1869.

42. Mob decoy from Harrodsburg hangs Geo Bolling, July 17, 1869.

43. Disguised band visited home of I.C. Vanarsdall and T.J. Vanarsdall in Mercer County, July 18, 1869.

44. Mob attacked Ronsey's house in Casey County. Three men and one woman were killed, July, 1869.

45. James Cowders—hung by a mob near Lebanon, Marion County, August 9, 1869.

46. Mob tarred and feathered a citizen of Cynthia in Harridan County, August, 1869.

47. Mob whipped and bruised a Negro in Davis County, September, 1869.

48. Ku Klux Klan burned colored meeting house in Carol County, September, 1869.

49. Ku Klux Klan whipped a Negro at John Carmine's farm in Fayette County, September, 1869.

50. Wiley Gevens—killed by Ku Klux Klan at Dixon, Webster County, October, 1869.

51. Geo Rose—killed by Ku Klux Klan near Kirkville in Madison County, October 18, 1869.

52. Ku Klux Klan ordered Wallace Sinkhorn to leave his home near Parkville, Boyle County, October, 1869.

53. A man named Sheperd was shot by a mob near Parksville, October, 1869.

54. Regulator killed Geo Tanhely in Lincoln County, November 2, 1869.

55. Ku Klux Klan attacked Frank Searcy's house in Madison County. One man was shot, November, 1869.

56. Searcy—hung by a mob in Madison County at Richmond, November 4, 1869.

57. Ku Klux Klan killed Robert Mershon. Daughter was shot, November, 1869.

58. Mob whipped Pope Hall and Willett in Washington County, November, 1869.

59. Regulators whipped Cooper in Pulaski County, November, 1869.

60. Ku Klux Klan ruffians outraged Negroes in Hickman County, November 20, 1869.

61. Mob takes two Negroes from jail in Richmond, Madison County. One was hung, one was whipped, December 12, 1869.

62. Two Negroes killed by a mob while in civil custody near Mayfield, Graves County, December, 1869.

63. Allen Cooper—killed by Ku Klux Klan in Adair County, December 24, 1869.

64. Negroes were whipped while on Scott's farm in Franklin County, December, 1869.

XVII.

SEPARATE BUT EQUAL
THE PLESSY V. FERGUSON DECISION[5]

M r. Justice Brown, after stating the facts in the foregoing language, delivered the opinion of the court.

This case turns upon the constitutionality of an act of the general assembly of the state of Louisiana, passed in 1890, providing for separate railway carriages for the white and colored races. Acts 1890, No. 111, p. 152.

The first section of the statute enacts "that all railway companies carrying passengers in their coaches in this state, shall provide equal but separate accommodations for the white and colored races, by providing two or more passenger coaches for each passenger train, or by dividing the passenger coaches by a partition so as to secure separate accommodations: provided,

---

5   163 U.S., 537 [1896]. Excerpts. Mr. Justice Harlan's dissent, omitted here for space reasons, termed the arbitrary separation of citizens on the basis of race a badge of servitude, inconsistent with the equality before the law established by the Thirteenth, Fourteenth, and Fifteenth Amendments to the Constitution.

that this section shall not be construed to apply to street rail-road. No person or persons shall be permitted to occupy seats in coaches, other than the ones assigned to them, on account the race they belong to. . . ."

The constitutionality of this act is attacked upon the grounds that it conflicts both with the Thirteenth Amendment of the constitution, abolishing slavery, and the Fourteenth Amendment, which prohibits certain restrictive legislation on the part of the states.

1. That it does not conflict with the Thirteenth Amendment, which abolished slavery and involuntary servitude, except as a punishment for crime, is too clear for argument. Slavery implies involuntary servitude, a state of bondage; the owner-ship of mankind as a chattel, or, at least, the control of the labor and services of one man for the benefit of another, and the absence of a legal right to the disposal of his own person, prop-erty, and services. This Amendment was said in the Slaughter-House Cases, 16 Wall. 36, to have been intended primarily to abolish slavery, as it had been previously known in this coun-try, and that it equally forbade Mexican peonage or the Chinese coolie trade, when they amounted to slavery or involuntary servitude, and that the use of the word "servitude" was intend-ed to prohibit the use of all forms of involuntary slavery, of whatever class or name. It was intimated, however, in that case, that this Amendment was regarded by the statesmen of that day as insufficient to protect the colored race from certain laws which had been enacted in the Southern states, imposing upon the colored race onerous disabilities and burdens, and curtail-ing their rights in the pursuit of life, liberty, and property to such an extent that their freedom was of little value; and that the Fourteenth Amendment was devised to meet this exigency.

So, too, in the Civil Rights Cases, 109 U.S. 3, 3 Sup. Ct. 18, it was said that the act of a mere individual, the owner of an inn, a public conveyance or place of amusement, refusing accommodations to colored people, cannot be justly regarded as imposing any badge of slavery or servitude upon the applicant, but only as involving an ordinary civil injury, properly cognizable by the laws of the state, and presumably subject to redress by those laws until the contrary appears. "It would be running the slavery question into the ground," said Mr. Justice Bradley, "to make it apply to every act of discrimination which a person may see fit to make as to the guests he will entertain, or as to the people he will take into his coach or cab or car, or admit to his concert or theater, or deal with in other matters of intercourse or business."

A statute which implies merely a legal distinction between the white and colored races—a distinction which is founded in the two races, and which must always exist so long as white men are distinguished from the other race by color—has no tendency to destroy the legal equality of the two races, or reestablish a state of involuntary servitude. Indeed, we do not understand that the Thirteenth Amendment is strenuously relied upon by the plaintiff in error in this connection.

2. By the Fourteenth Amendment, all persons born or naturalized in the United States, and subject to the jurisdiction thereof, are made citizens of the United States and of the state wherein they reside; and the states are forbidden from making or enforcing any law which shall abridge the privileges or immunities of citizens of the United States, or shall deprive any person of life, liberty, or property without due process of law, or deny to any person within their jurisdiction the equal protection of the laws. . . .

141

The object of the Amendment was undoubtedly to enforce the absolute equality of the two races before the law, but, in the nature of things, it could not have been intended to abolish distinctions based upon color, to enforce social, as distinguished from political, equality, or a commingling of the two races upon terms unsatisfactory to either. Laws permitting, and even requiring, their separation, in places where they are liable to be brought into contact, do not necessarily imply the inferiority of either race to the other, and have been generally, if not universally, recognized as within the competency of the state legislatures in the exercise of their police power. The most common instance of this is connected with the establishment of separate schools for white and colored children, which have been held to be a valid exercise of the legislative power even by courts of states where the political rights of the colored race have been longest and most earnestly enforced.

One of the earliest of these cases is that of Roberts v. City of Boston, 5 Cush. 198, in which the supreme judicial court of Massachusetts held that the general school committee of Boston had power to make provision for the instruction of colored children in separate schools established exclusively for them, and to prohibit their attendance upon the other schools. "The great principle," said Chief Justice Shaw, "advanced by the learned and eloquent advocate for the plaintiff [Mr. Charles Summer], is that, by the constitution and laws of Massachusetts, all persons, without distinction of age or sex, birth or color, origin or condition, are equal before the law. . . . But, when this great principle comes to be applied to the actual and various conditions of persons in society, it will not warrant the assertion that men and women are legally clothed with the same civil and political powers, and that children and adults are legally to have the same functions and be subject to the same treatment; but only that the rights of all, as they are settled and regulated by law, are equally entitled to the paternal consideration and protection of the law for their maintenance and security." It was held that the powers of the committee extended to the establishment of separate schools for children of different ages, sexes and colors, and that they might also establish special schools for poor and neglected children, who have become too old to attend the primary school, and yet have not acquired the rudiment of learning, to enable them to enter the ordinary schools. . . It is also suggested by the learned counsel for the plaintiff in error that the same argument that will justify the state legislature in requiring railways to provide separate accommodations for the two races will also authorize them to require separate cars to be provided for people whose hair is of a certain color, or who are aliens, or who belong to certain nationalities, or to enact laws requiring colored people to walk upon one side of the street, and white people upon the other, or requiring white men's houses to be painted white, and colored men's black, or their vehicles or business signs to be different colors, upon the theory that one side of the street is as good as one of another color. The reply to all this is that every exercise of the public good, and not for the annoyance or oppression of a particular class. . . .

So far, then, as a conflict with the Fourteenth Amendment is concerned, the case reduces itself to the question whether the statute of Louisiana is a reasonable regulation, and with respect to this there must necessarily be a large discretion on the part of the legislature. In determining the question of reasonableness, it is at liberty to act with reference to the established usages, customs, and traditions of the people, and with a view to the promotion of their comfort, and the preservation of the public peace and good order. Gauged by this standard we cannot say that a law which authorizes or even requires the separation of the two races in public conveyances is unreasonable, or more obnoxious to the Fourteenth Amendment than the acts of congress requiring separate schools for colored children in the District of Columbia, the constitutionality of which does not seem to have been questioned, or the corresponding acts of state legislatures.

We consider the underlying fallacy of the plaintiff's argument to consist in the assumption that the enforced separation of the two races stamps the colored race with a badge of inferiority. If this be so, it is not by reason of anything found in the act, but solely because the colored race chooses to put that construction upon it. The argument necessarily assumes that if—as has been more than once the case, and is not unlikely to be so again—the colored race should become the dominant power in the state legislature, and should enact a law in precisely similar term, it would thereby relegate the white race to an inferior position. We imagine that the white race, at least, would not acquiesce in this assumption. The argument also assumes that social prejudices may be overcome by legislation, and that equal rights cannot be secured to the negro except by an enforced commingling of the two races. We cannot accept this proposition. If the two races are to meet upon terms of social equality, it must be the results of natural affinities, a mutual appreciation of each other's merits, and a voluntary consent of individuals. . . .

XVIII.

A.M.E.'S PARTICIPATION IN THE CIVIL RIGHTS STRUGGLE

To fully understand A.M.E.'s participation in the movement of human rights, we must turn to "the other side of 1965."

December 1, 1955: Mrs. Rosa Parks, a Negro woman, boarded a bus in Montgomery, Alabama, to ride home. Mrs. Parks was a member of St. Paul A.M.E. Church, where she was a member of the choir and the Stewardess Board and was involved in many other activities of her church. She was undoubtedly impressed by the independent spirit displayed by Richard Allen, and his stand for human dignity and respect. Once a year in her church and all other A.M.E. churches throughout the connection, on Founders Day, the second Sunday in February, the life of Richard Allen is emphasized, along with his refusal to accept prescribed seats in St. George's Church in Philadelphia, Pennsylvania. His refusal and his walking out and organizing the A.M.E. church as a protest against segregation and unfair treatment of Negroes is driven home to all A.M.E. churches. Mrs. Rosa Parks had a built-up philosophy of independence, a respect for human dignity, and a belief that God respects all persons alike.

An event may not just happen overnight. It is usually developed from a long history of meditation and thoughts on the part of the individual. So, when Mrs. Rosa Parks was told by the bus driver to get up and give her seat to a white male passenger, she refused. Three other Negroes obeyed the bus driver and moved. Mrs. Parks refused and was arrested and jailed.

Her refusal brought to a head a list of long dissatisfactions, which Negroes had suffered in Montgomery, Alabama, the so-called cradle of the confederacy. In a mass meeting, Negroes decided to walk rather than suffer indignities. The slogan was, "Walk in dignity rather than ride in shame." This incident, and the results that followed, showed the white south that they had to deal with a new Negro. Reverend R.W. Hilson, a leading A.M.E. pastor in Montgomery, as well as the pastor of St. John A.M.E. Church of Montgomery, Alabama, called on other A.M.E.'s to support the boycott, and the built-up sentiment both in the state and elsewhere.

Reverend Hilson was the first to suggest retaliation for the insults heaped upon Mrs. Rosa Parks, and aided in organizing an effective boycott. He was a prime mover in mapping out the strategy and details for the entire movement. His van was used in the car pool that lasted for a year. He was called upon to give both his time and money. As state leader for the Ninth Episcopal District, he encouraged the entire state to stand firm and not be moved on the issue of human dignity, since the entire church was built upon a philosophy of respect for personality and human dignity. He, like Rosa Parks, was one of the heroes of the success of the Montgomery boycott. I was glad to see the Congress and the President honor her recently, and to see Saint Paul A.M.E. Church in Montgomery, where Reverend Joseph

Rembert is pastor, name and dedicate a chapel in honor of Mrs. Rosa Parks. The incident of Mrs. Rosa Parks' refusal to be kicked around on the bus in Montgomery elevated the late Dr. Martin Luther King Jr to both national and international fame, leading to the creation of the Southern Christian Leadership Conference. This organization has accomplished much for Negroes in gaining our civil rights and has aided in awakening the world to the so-called Negro problem.

The bus boycott lasted a year starting on December 1, 1955 and ended December 20, 1956. The Negroes returned to riding the buses unsegregated, and there were only a few isolated incidents that occurred. Not only are Negroes riding in the front, middle, and back with freedom of choice, or first come first served, but in many instances, Negroes are in the driver's seat.

The contribution of Mrs. Rosa Parks to subsequent civil rights accomplishments is often overlooked or not even mentioned. That her great inspiration to stand up for human dignity came from her church can hardly be questioned. The extent to which the Negro race and the country as a whole owe a debt of gratitude to Mrs. Rosa Parks will never be adequately measured. "She indeed lit the fuse for the movement." It should never be forgotten that Mrs. Rosa Parks furnished the sinews, the raw material out of which the Negro bus boycott had its origin. From this beginning, many legislative enactments for the benefit of the Negro people throughout the world followed.

Ten Students at an A.M.E. College
Stage a Sit-in, in Birmingham, Alabama

Ten students from Daniel Payne College, Thursday, April, 1960, at 10:30 a.m., entered five Whites only department stores. All were arrested and kept in jail overnight. Bear in mind that this confrontation against segregation by the students registered in Daniel Payne College, an A.M.E. institution, began three years before the Birmingham confrontation in 1963, which reached national and international proportion. Shortly after this sit-in by the students of Daniel Payne College, the United Press International carried the following article:

Police Report Cross Burning

Birmingham, Alabama, was the focal point of a widespread series of cross burnings. The police reported that about thirty crosses were set afire within an hour in Birmingham and in the immediate suburbs and towns. One was set afire in front of the Daniel Payne College for Negroes.

Three years after the sit-in by Payne College students in April, 1963, a Negro leader decided to sue for all citizens for the removal of all restrictions in snack-bars, department stores, and to upgrade hiring policies for Negroes in Birmingham. This brought on vital confrontations in 1963, but this was three years after the sit-in of the students of Daniel Payne College in 1960. All actions were met with arrests by Public Safety Director Eugene Bull Conner, who was known for his hardline tactics. Birmingham at this time had city ordinances against mixing of the races, and adhered to strict segregation laws, and anyone who ran counter to these statutes subjected himself to arrest, a sentence, or a fine—or both. As the Negroes demonstrated and sang freedom songs, the Public Safety Director ordered their arrest, using paddy wagons, school buses and other vehicles. Hundreds upon hundreds were arrested, seemingly in an atmosphere of non-violence as preached by the Southern Christian Leadership Conference.

On May 3, however, the shock came. As the demonstrators started marching, a powerful stream of water from a fire hydrant was turned on the student demonstrators, which knocked them to the ground. Some students were bitten by gaping police dogs eager to get away from their leashes. The picture of these police dogs and a knocking to the ground of students by swift fire hoses attracted world-wide attention when they appeared in the national papers.

In retaliation to these acts of violence on the part of the police department, Negroes threw rocks and bottles, and this really precipitated the so-called Birmingham riot. With dogs and the fire hoses, the police were able to control to an extent the demonstrators, but the incidents gave Birmingham a picture of cruelty, which it will take many years to overcome.

It was necessary for the Justice Department to send representatives to Birmingham, and their arrival had a great impact. During the following weeks, more than twenty-five-hundred were arrested, and officials boasted that they had plenty of room for more.

In May of 1963, the A.G. Gaston Motel was bombed, leaving a large hole in the side of the wall. This was the room where the late Dr. Martin Luther King Jr stayed on his visits to Birmingham. Dr. A.G. Gaston was a life-long member of the A.M.E. church and a bulwark in funding money to bail demonstrators and practically all civil rights workers out of jail. He bailed out both Dr. Martin Luther King and Reverend David Abernathy when the bail was increased to two thousand five hundred dollars each. Dr. Gaston's motel was really the strategy headquarters for the civil rights movement in Birmingham, and plans for the demonstrations and sit-ins were arranged in these quarters. It became necessary for the President of the United States to dispatch troops to strategic positions near Birmingham. The President made it clear

149

in a speech that racial struggle in the city of Birmingham could not lead to further bloodshed or brutal repression.

The entire world was shocked when four little young lives were wiped out by a bomb in the 16th Street Baptist Church in Birmingham. I am happy to report that, after thirty-seven years, the long arm of the law alleged that they caught two men who murdered those innocent young people. You can run but you can't hide. You may feel that you have gotten by, but you have not gotten away. *What's done in the dark will one day come to the light. Be not deceived, God is not mocked, whatsoever a man or woman sow that shall he or she also reap. Remember God sees us all.*

Letters to Reverend J.A. DeLaine

The Supreme Court decision to outlaw school desegregation was handed down May 17, 1954. Five years prior to this day, the Reverend J.A. DeLaine, an A.M.E. preacher, hurled the first serious blow in that time against this systemic evil of school segregation, as the letter below will show.

Harold R. Boulware
Attorney at Law
1109 1/2 Washington Street
Columbia, South Carolina
March 8, 1949

Reverend J.A. DeLaine
Summerton, South Carolina

Dear Reverend DeLaine:

Thurgood Marshall and the legal staff are having a meeting here in Columbia on March 12, 1949, at 10 o'clock in the Palmetto State Teacher's building for the purpose of mapping out plans for our school action. It is my hope that you will be able to come to this meeting and that you can help us with all the information regarding Claredon County. Bring whoever you can.

Very truly yours,
Harold R. Boulware

This letter shows that Reverend DeLaine started the desegregation fight and had secured cooperation from the National NAACP in his home state, South Carolina. This was five years before the Supreme Court decision. The letter below, on the bus transportation suit, shows that all forms of school segregation were being attacked, including transportation.

South Carolina State Conference of the NAACP State office
Columbia, South Carolina
February 10, 1948

Dear Reverend DeLaine:

The check for $83.20 from you came today. Many thanks for the same. It has been deposited to the account of the defense fund of the NAACP. The legal papers in the school bus transportation case have been drawn and are in the National Office for checking. We expect them back any day.

The school district members have granted a hearing to Attorney Boulware on Friday, February 27, 1948. Mr. Boulware is requesting you to meet him there. You will hear from him on this matter. It has taken a long time to get to the case, but we are now about ready for filing. We will call on the people for support, and we will reimburse you for your expenses.

Yours very truly,
James M. Hinton, President
State Chapter NAACP

This letter shows that Reverend DeLaine had advanced his personal funds to get a movement started, which would benefit the children of his county and undoubtedly would serve as a pattern for the entire country. These preliminary activities on the local level were necessary, and resulted in the first school desegregation case to reach the federal courts in the year 1951. This case from Claredon County, South Carolina, was brought by an A.M.E. church. The fight was actually started in Claredon, South Carolina, by A.M.E. preachers.

The three-judge federal court in South Carolina upheld the constitutionality of the separate-but-equal doctrine by a vote of 2-1, but ordered action to correct evident inequality of Negro schools in the state of South Carolina.

A native of the state was harassed, threatened and later driven out of the state because of his courageous stand on this and other historical questions. The same is true of Reverend J.A. DeLaine. The difference was that in the case of Reverend DeLaine, his church and home were burned to the ground, his personal property dissipated, but he was able to keep body and soul together.

On January 28, 1952, this Claredon case finally reached the Supreme Court of the United States, and even that august body acted seemingly in a way to avoid a direct confrontation in this all-important case. The case was sent back to the lower court with a request that a report be made on the date filed by the school board concerning the program to equalize facilities for Negro and white students. Two of the justices dissented—Justice Hugo Black, originally an Alabaman, and Justice William O'Douglas. They took the position that the report from the school board on the progress made to equalize facilities was irrelevant and not necessarily a part of the broad constitutional question involved, and suggested that the question based upon the protection clause of the United States Constitution be argued at once.

In the fall of 1952, this case was back again in the Supreme Court, along with other cases from Delaware, the District of Columbia, Virginia, and Kansas. It is undoubtedly true that this fight started in Claredon County, South Carolina, back in 1948-49. As the letters above show, and wide publicity given to happenings in these deep southern states encouraged others to begin a similar fight in their areas.

Black folks should never forget Judge J. Waiters' warning, the first federal judge in modern history to dissent on this all-important question of Negro rights. And we should recall with admiration the dissenting opinions of Supreme Court Justices Hugo Black and William O'Douglas. This famous decision reemphasized the purposes of the Fourteenth Amendment, namely, to guarantee to Negroes full and complete equality before the law and to abolish all legal distinctions based on color of skin or race. The court held that the Fourteenth Amendment to the United States Constitution barred all forms of segregation based on color of skin and previous conditions of servitude.

Brown v. Topeka, Kansas, Board of Education

The case of Brown against the Topeka, Kansas, Board of Education was the first such case to come before the United

States Supreme Court. Reverend Oliver Leon Brown was also an A.M.E. preacher. Reverend Brown filed suit against the Topeka Board of Education on behalf of his nine-year-old daughter, Linda, who had to walk five blocks to catch a school bus and then ride two miles to an all-Negro school, while there was an all-White school only four and a half blocks from her home.

This case was argued in the Kansas Supreme Court and then reached the U.S. Supreme Court. This famous decision eventually led to the integration of public schools throughout the nation.

Reverend Brown displayed great courage in pushing this case, not only for his nine-year-old daughter, but for all Negro children. While honor is certainly due to the NAACP for using its talent and know-how, it is often forgotten that the spade-work must be done down in the local community before the NAACP, S.C.L.C., or any other national organization can even begin its task. Many local leaders spent nights and days in meetings, and covering the entire region without pay, consoling the upset of the entire region and fearful persons, singling out plaintiffs and encouraging solidarity of Negroes before any headway could be made. The local people defied threats of reprisals, danger and even death in order to get the movement up off the ground.

Reverend A.T. Days who was pastoring St. Matthews A.M.E. Church in Greensboro, Alabama, along with his wife, opened the doors of the church in the sixties. His church was burned and his house was shot into during those turbulent days. Had it not been for people like Albert Turner, James Orange, and others, we would not have made it. They said, like Richard Allen hundreds of years ago, "We shall never turn back," and we didn't, and we won the victory. After the passing of the

154

Voting Rights Bill, we were able to register thousands of black folks who had not been able to register before.

Support from the A.M.E. Church
Across the Connection

In the First District, the Bishop met with committees, planned strategic aid and was one of the first to openly espouse the cause of poor Negroes in the Southland who were battling against tremendous odds. Bishop Bright took the position that, while publicized violence threw the spotlight on Georgia, Alabama, and Mississippi, Negroes in large northern cities faced problems more subtle and perhaps as acute as those in the South. He used the power of his office to help the ghetto Negroes in the entire First Episcopal District, especially in Philadelphia, New York City, Boston, and Buffalo. In both Philadelphia and New York, he served on important committees in an effort to keep the cities cool as well as to gain additional rights and opportunities for Negroes. When the call came to support the Selma to Montgomery march, Bishop Bright chartered three planes, and a large delegation from the First District flew to Alabama and participated in this dangerous confrontation with Governor Wallace.

In the Second Episcopal District, Bishop George W. Baber was one of the closest Negroes to the White House and served with the Director of Minorities to advise President Johnson on bills which ought to be passed to alleviate racial tension and at the same time help Negroes throughout the country. His influence was thus far-reaching and significant. After the death of Martin Luther King Jr and during the Washington riots, along with Mr. Martin, Director of Minorities, Roy Wilkins of the NAACP and Bishop Baber were called to the White House by

President Johnson for a confidential small but significant conference.

After much discussion, the President asked point blank, "Bishop Baber, what steps do you think should be taken?"

Bishop Baber replied, "Mr. President, to quote an old familiar saying, it is better to do the best things possible during the worst possible times." The President, along with Vice President Humphrey, seized upon this expression, which colored all subsequent round-table discussions and resulted in the President calling in important Congressional leaders whom he urged to pass the 1968 Civil Rights Bill at once.

This certainly alleviated some tension throughout the country. Bishop Baber, on his frequent visits to the White House after 1964, had great weight in the passage of other bills, including the 1964 and 1965 Civil Rights Bill as well as others affecting the welfare of Negroes. He was somewhat of an unheralded secret adviser to the President of the United States on matters affecting black people. It is probably true that he was more of a confidential adviser to President Johnson than any other previous Bishop who presided over the Second Episcopal District.

In the Third Episcopal District, Bishop Wilkes, though busy with the reorganization of the greater Wilberforce University, used his position of influence to aid Negroes in their struggles, especially in large cities like Cleveland, Cincinnati, Columbus, Dayton, Pittsburgh, and Toledo. The weight of his office as well as that of A.M.E. churches in the district was thrown behind the candidacy of Mr. Stokes, and he became the first Negro mayor elected in a major American city. Bishop Wilkes has always believed in political power as a means of rectifying social ills and is a true follower of Turiner, Flipper, Fountain, and others of Georgia fame. Therefore, he stepped out into the forefront

156

when the interest of the Negro was at stake. Great financial aid was rendered from large churches in the Third Episcopal District, which Bishop Wilkes visited and delivered to the South during the period of great tension and confrontation.

In the Fourth Episcopal District many ministers as well as the Bishop made trips to the South carrying large sums of money to aid Negroes in Alabama and Mississippi. Bishop Gomez used his office to serve on important committees in Chicago, Detroit and other large cities to map strategy and plan conferences to help Negroes gain a greater share of the good things of life in places where these opportunities were denied. Bishop Gomez, a very forceful platform orator, frequently called the attention of influential white audiences to the injustices suffered by Negroes and the frustration which any group similarly situated would face. His appearances before significant and influential audiences allowed the entire Mid-western section of the country to know where the A.M.E. church stood in the current Negro revolt.

In the Fifth Episcopal District, Bishop Primm lit the spark, which fired up both Negroes and Whites to take an interest in the struggles of Negroes in Mississippi and Alabama. Large sums of money were raised throughout the District and sent to bail Negroes out of jail in Mississippi and Alabama. On more than one occasion the Bishop himself headed delegations who brought sums of money to both Alabama and Mississippi.

In Los Angeles, he supported the efforts of Dr. Brookins (now a Bishop), Dr. Murph (now a Bishop), Dr. Ford, and others in far-away Seattle, Washington. He supported Dr. John Adams, who waged a bitter struggle to secure more opportunities for Negroes. In the entire Fifth Episcopal District, large cities like Los Angeles, Oakland, San Francisco, St Louis, Kansas City, Denver, and others, Bishop Primm, admonished his preachers to hold the line, and emphasized the fact that this fight involved not only Negroes in Alabama, Mississippi and Georgia, but Negroes all over the country. Dr. Brookins, Dr. Murph, Dr. Ford, and others of Los Angeles not only rendered great aid to Negroes during the Watts confrontation, but also made more than one trip with Bishop Primm to the Deep South, where the turmoil was raging. A.M.E. members of St. Louis, Kansas City, and other large centers in the Fifth District supported Bishop Primm in his efforts by contributing both their presence and money. In the Selma to Montgomery march, a very large delegation from the Fifth District, both White and Colored, accompanied Bishop Primm to Alabama to take part in this dangerous trek. Bishop Primm led the prayer on the steps of Brown Chapel A.M.E. Church before the final march from Selma to Montgomery. He also participated in the march on "Bloody Sunday."

In the Sixth Episcopal District, where much of the confrontation centered, Bishop Hickman stood firm for the rights of Negroes, even though he lived in Georgia. Bear in mind that it is one thing to fight in New York and Chicago, but is an entirely different story to stand firm in Georgia and Mississippi and Alabama, where mobs were running amok almost without any fear of being apprehended.

One of the preachers in Waycross, Georgia, literally opened every phase of that city's facilities to Negroes through boycotts, protests, and confrontations, and he received full support from his Bishop in his activities. The Morris-Brown student body participated in marches and confrontations in Atlanta, and the President of Morris-Brown, Dr. Middleton, and Bishop Hickman, Chairman of the Trustee Board, took the position that Morris-Brown could not punish students for taking whatever means they decided appropriate to gain their civil rights. Remember that this stand was taken at a time when Bishop Hickman and Middleton were seeking funds locally to build a greater Morris-Brown College.

158

In the Seventh Episcopal District, Bishop Gibbs stood firm for the rights of Negroes in South Carolina to enjoy any privilege that anyone else enjoyed. The students of Allen University marched, demonstrated and even tested the administrative policies of the University of South Carolina, situated also in Columbia. And Bishop Gibbs, although at the time seeking accreditation for Allen University, and seeking the support of local education interests, took the position that Negroes had been mistreated in South Carolina throughout the years, and if they decided to relieve the pressure from their backs, he would be the first to help them do so.

Bishop Gibbs in Florida, and in Alabama before going to South Carolina, was always forthright in demanding civil rights for his people, and has always felt that students had a right to oppose ideas they felt should be opposed. Bishop Gibbs, a former college president, has always been sympathetic to student problems.

The Allen University students, who led in the confrontation in South Carolina, found ready support from the president of the college and Bishop Gibbs in their stand for what they felt Negroes should receive.

Bishop W.F. Ball of the Eighth District allowed all people to know that in the civil rights struggle, the A.M.E. church, with all of its resources, stood silently behind those who were contending for this right.

Bishop Ball has always been a fighter, even while running for the office of Bishop, and South Carolina was fortunate to have him as their leader during this critical period. He would stand firm and not be moved on the question of civil rights for Negroes.

In the Eighth Episcopal District, both Bishop Jordan and the late Bishop Sims, in the heat of the struggle, allowed the people of Mississippi and Louisiana to know where the A.M.E.

church stood in the current Negro revolution. In Mississippi, entrenched evil, as it were, was in high places, and the governor himself was preaching defiance of the Supreme Court decision outlawing school segregation. In spite of this fact, the A.M.E. church under the leadership of these Bishops placed the might of the A.M.E. churches both Mississippi and Louisiana on the side of the people in their struggle for their rights. It should be remembered that the history of Bishop Jordan, even before his elevation, was that of a strong fighter for civil rights.

The Ninth Episcopal District, perhaps more than any other, bore the brunt of the civil rights struggle. Bishop I.H. Bonner used his personal funds to help bail Negroes out of jail, and also allowed Brown Chapel A.M.E. Church, to serve as headquarters for the Selma to Montgomery march. Bear in mind that this church is on the same street, as, and not far from, the home of Bishop Bonner. The Bishop, like many others, always faced danger because in Selma, Alabama, at this time, beatings and even murders were almost a daily occurrence.

Bishop Bonner was also Chairman of the Trustee Board of Daniel Payne College. Although the students of the college as far back as 1960 were being arrested for attempting to break segregation barriers in downtown Birmingham, Bishop Bonner supported their efforts, and it was never an issue for the Trustee Board over which he presided.

In the Tenth Episcopal District, Bishop O.L. Sherman had a record of standing up for Negroes in Arkansas, Oklahoma, and Texas. In the early years of the struggle for civil rights, Bishop Sherman allowed all to know where he stood on the issue, and used the weight of his office to gain consideration for Negroes on all issues affecting their welfare.

While the State of Texas was still trying to carry out the Supreme Court decision of 1954, Bishop Sherman served on

160

state committees seeking to ease the transition from inequality to full equality for all Negroes throughout the state. His ministers were admonished to stand firm, and not compromise any issue which would deny the Negroes their full equality as American citizens.

While confronted with the problems of rebuilding Paul Quinn College, and needing local white support, he nevertheless allowed all to know that, regardless of consequences, his people deserved and should have full and equal rights as any other citizen in America.

In the Eleventh Episcopal District, the late Bishop E.C. Hatcher and his eminent successor Bishop George N. Collins stood firm for civil rights for Negroes in the state of Florida.

The record of Bishop Collins in the hotbed of the civil rights struggle in the Twelfth District, embracing the State of Arkansas, preceded him to the State of Florida, his home state. There has never been any question as to his stand on the issue of full equality for Negroes in America. Remember that it was in Arkansas where the famous Little Rock Nine faced howling mobs. Six of the nine, who were determined to implement the Supreme Court decision of 1954 and enter Central High School in Little Rock, were members of A.M.E. churches in the city, as was Daisy Bates, sponsor of the group.

It can be said in passing that even in his campaign for the high office of Bishop, Dr. Collins expressed himself as believing that Negroes should continue to fight for full equality, and asserted often in his speeches that "he who would be free" must himself strike the first blow.

In the Twelfth District to an extent efforts merged with those of the Eleventh, due to the death of Bishop Hatcher. Bishop Collins transferred from the Twelfth to the Eleventh District. The change was significant as Bishop D. Ward Nichols followed Bishop Collins to this hotbed of racial confrontation. Fortunately for our church, Bishop Nichols was a close confidant of Governor Rockefeller of New York, whose brother was governor of Arkansas and a leading force for the entire region. Letters were exchanged between the two brothers, and Bishop Nichols had a receptive ear on matters affecting our people, especially in the State of Arkansas, where the problems were extremely acute.

Bishop Nichols has a record of not compromising on any issue when it comes to the rights of his people, and, regardless of consequences, he has been known to be immovable, and to stand firm when it was not popular to take a stand and speak out. Bishop Nichols used his high office and unusual connections in national bodies to get them to recognize the growing concern of racism in American society. His record throughout life is one of a constant fight for the rights of his people.

In the Thirteenth Episcopal District, the final home district of the A.M.E. church, Bishop Hickman and Bishop Jordan were both influential in supporting every effort of our people designed to gain their civil rights. They encouraged ministers to take a stand on every civil rights issue, and in the Louisville, Nashville, Chattanooga, and Memphis confrontations, they gave invaluable support to marches and demonstrations in an effort to call the country's attention to the injustices suffered by our people. Although the Thirteenth Episcopal District may not have given the appearance of being as violent as Alabama or Mississippi, there were indeed several problems in the area, which needed and received the wise counsel of the A.M.E. Episcopal leaders. Indeed, it may be said that in the thirteen home districts of the A.M.E. church, all Bishops carried out the true philosophy of Richard Allen, and stood up and were counted when it came to the questions of injustice and unfair treatment of Negroes in the United States of America.

XIX.

A LOOK AT THE PAST

In 1888, at the celebration of the centennial of the first settlement in Ohio at Marietta, a black man, B.W. Arnett, said, "The Northwest Territory to us was the land of Canaan, the promise of liberty, of honey and milk and wine." In 1885, Greene County voters had elected Arnett as state representative and sent him to the 67th session of the Ohio state legislature for a two-year term, 1886-1887. Arnett's candidacy had been announced in the November 18, 1884, edition of the *Xenia Gazette*. Later, a committee headed by James P. Shorter of Wilberforce informed *Gazette* readers that Arnett had made thirty-two speeches in 1872 for Ulysses S. Grant, that he had "stumped the state" for Rutherford B. Hayes and James A. Garfield, and supported other candidates as well.

Arnett won the Republican nomination for state representative in the Greene County primary by edging out John B. Allen of Spring Valley and Horace Ankeney of Xenia. The vote was Arnett 1,683, Allen 1,666 and Ankeney 1,117. Tuesday, October 8, 1885, John B. Allen noted that there had been an attempt following the primary to prejudice people against

Arnett because of his color. Allen asked that all Republicans support him because he was worthy and fitted for the position. The Republicans supported him and carried fifteen of the twenty precincts in the county. The official results of the October 13 election were printed in the *Gazette* on October 16: Arnett 4,326, his opponent C. Darlington 2,386.

Benjamin Arnett was no stranger to politics. His political activities began in 1864 when he joined the National Equal Rights League in Syracuse, New York. Prior to that time he had organized several societies in Brownsville, including the Sons of Hannibal and the Mutual Aid Society in 1859. His outstanding oratorical skills brought him an invitation to speak at the Centennial Celebration of the First Settlement of the Northwest Territory at Marietta in 1888.

Benjamin William Arnett was born March 6, 1838, in Brownsville, Fayette County, Pennsylvania, the son of Samuel and Mary Arnett. As a young man he worked on steamboats on the Ohio and Monongahela Rivers. Arnett obtained a teaching certificate and taught school. He was licensed to preach in the African Methodist Episcopal Church in 1865, ordained a deacon by Bishop Paul Quinn in 1868, and ordained an elder in 1870 by Daniel A. Payne in Xenia. He was elected the seventh Bishop of the A.M.E. church in 1888. As a member of the Ohio legislature, he authored the bill abolishing the "black laws" (laws which limited the rights of black citizens). He became a lifelong friend of William McKinley.

When McKinley took the oath of office as President of the United States on March 4, 1897, the Bible he used was presented to him by Bishop Arnett on behalf of the A.M.E. church. In addition to his career as a statesman, church leader, educator, powerful orator, and author, he was trustee and life member of the Ohio Archeological and Historical Society. He figured importantly in the history of Payne Theological Seminary, Wilberforce University, and its Combined Normal and Industrial Department—now Central State University—and the A.M.E. church. As editor of the budget, he included biographical sketches, sermons, statistics, and much information on black Americans and organizations other than A.M.E. in those publications. His home at Wilberforce "Tawawa Chimney Corners" was located near the old Indian Tawawa Springs. It later became the home of the late Bishop Reverdy C. Ransom. B.W. Arnett died of uremic poisoning at Wilberforce, October 9, 1906.

XX.

IN PURSUIT OF FREEDOM

For three centuries, Negroes in the United States have been struggling for freedom. It is not true that they were satisfied with bondage and that they put forth no efforts to emancipate themselves. There is plenty of evidence to show that many slaves were not loyal to their masters to the very end. There are also data to prove that there were slaves who did everything in their power to destroy the slave system and free themselves from it. Even onboard ship, there were instances of rebellion before the cargoes reached America. Hughes and Meltzer point out that, "On the *Kentucky*, more than forty slaves were once put to death for staging an uprising in mid- ocean."[1] How many Africans were killed en route to America because they staged rebellions, we have no way of knowing. It is estimated that 20 percent of those Africans brought to America died en route. Foul air, stagnant water and spoiled food killed many. Some who rebelled were shot and some committed suicide.

---

[1] Delivered at the Interdemoninational Theological Center, Atlanta, Georgia, celebrating the Centinnial of the Emancipation Proclamation.

Negroes began to register their disapproval of being held in bondage in Virginia as early as 1663. From that time on up to and through the Civil War, the Negro slaves attempted to travel many paths to freedom. Among them were: insurrections, running away, organized efforts through the underground railroad, purchasing their freedom, pleading their cause by preaching and praying, speaking, and writing, deserting to the British in the Revolutionary Army, seeking relief by committing suicide, fighting in the Union Army, advocating colonization, and petitioning the Government. Virginia began to fear the uprising of slaves as early as 1663. John Hope Franklin wrote the following:

> Virginia had real reason to fear the Negro population, for as early as 1663, the slaves gave evidence of being restive under their yoke and began conspiring to rebel against their masters. In the following decades, there was open discontent among the slaves in several sections of the colony. In 1687, a plot was uncovered in the Northern Neck in which the slaves, during a mass funeral, had planned to kill all the whites in the vicinity in a desperate bid for freedom. By 1694, lawlessness among the slaves had become so widespread that Governor Andros complained that there was insufficient enforcement of the code.

In 1770, near Charleston, South Carolina, several slaves were burned alive and others banished because they were accused of planning a revolt. There was another uprising in 1730, and in 1739 there were three uprisings in South Carolina. In that year, slaves killed the guards in a warehouse, took arms and ammunition, and set out toward Florida. Other Negroes joined them in the march and killed all white persons who interfered with them.

167

The slaves did not succeed. They were pursued and captured, and many slaves and white people were killed. The next year, 1740, in a conspiracy of two hundred Negroes, fifty were captured and hanged.

New York experienced an organized insurrection in 1712. Negroes armed themselves with guns, knives, and hatchets in an orchard close to the center of town. A slave set fire to his master's outhouse for the purpose of attracting white people to the scene so that they could be shot down by the armed Negroes. The state militia was called out and the Negroes sought refuge in the woods. Several of them, rather than be captured, committed suicide. Several cut their own throats, and one man shot his wife and then shot himself. Twenty slaves were executed. Some were hanged, some burned alive, one was hanged by the chin and allowed to die without food or drink, and one was broken on the wheel.

There were revolts in Louisiana in 1795. Perhaps the most widely known attempts to free the slaves were the insurrections of Denmark Vesey of South Carolina and Nat Turner of Virginia. Vesey purchased his freedom in 1800, years before his attempted uprising in 1822. The second Sunday in July, 1822, was the date set for the insurrection. He had his colleagues scattered for several miles around Charleston ready to strike on the appointed day. But his plans leaked out and Vesey attempted to postpone the revolt.

Word of the postponement did not get around. More than a hundred slaves were arrested, and of this number, forty-seven were condemned. It is estimated that Vesey had involved approximately nine thousand in the planned revolt. Vesey and thirty-six others were put to death.

Nine years after the abortive efforts of Denmark Vesey, Nat Turner of Virginia staged the greatest revolt of all. He was a plowman and a preacher. His father before him had escaped to freedom. Turner believed he was called of God to set his people free. His plan was to kill all Whites on the nearest plantation, expecting to gather followers as he went along. Turner started his revolt on August 13, 1831. He and his followers began by killing his master, Joseph Travis, and his family. In a short span of twenty-four hours, sixty Whites were killed. The revolt succeeded well until the Negroes were overpowered by state and federal troops. More than a hundred slaves were killed in the encounter. Nat himself was executed on November 11, 1831.

The fact that many Negroes deserted to the British Army during the Revolutionary War is proof that they did so because it was announced British policy that if slaves joined the British Army, they would be set free. This policy, however, changed the attitude of the colonists and they enlisted slaves for the American Army. Massachusetts and Rhode Island allowed slaves to serve in the Revolutionary War as early as 1778. Washington is reputed to have had five thousand Negroes, free and slaves, under his command. Negroes fought as all-Negro units from Massachusetts, Rhode Island, and Connecticut, but in the North and South, Negroes were integrated into fighting forces with Whites. South Carolina refused to enlist slaves, and it is estimated that some twenty-five thousand South Carolina slaves escaped to British lines. In Georgia, at the siege of Augusta, about a third of the men manning Fort Cornwallis for the British were runaway slaves who were not acceptable on the American side.

Several individual Negroes won distinction in the Continental Army. Peter Salem became a hero when he shot British Major Pitcairn at the Battle of Bunker Hill in 1775. Salem Poor won recognition as a gallant soldier. There is Black Sampson who, at the Battle of Brandywine in 1777, armed with a scythe, performed "great deeds of valor." In 1777, a black soldier, Tack Sisson, assisted in the capture of General Prescott. A year later at The Battle of Rhode Island, a Negro regiment three times beat back Hessian troops. A black spy, called Pompey, is given credit for supplying information which led to the victory at Stony Point in 1779. Two years later, a unit of Negro soldiers was destroyed defending Colonel Green at Points Bridge, New York. These data are sufficient to prove that Negroes pursued devious paths in their efforts to be free.

The Underground Railroad is another path used by Negroes to free themselves. Abolitionists and free Negroes made a strong attack on the institution of slavery through the Underground Railroad. Harriet Tubman is perhaps the most outstanding of the Negro conductors on the Underground Railroad. She escaped from slavery herself and led many slaves to freedom. With her frail body, she might have folded her hands and done nothing. But she is reputed to have gone south nineteen times and freed more than 300 slaves. She took no foolishness. A story is told of the slaves who got weary and turned back to slave land. After that Harnet Tubman purchased a pistol. She threatened to shoot the next slave who attempted to turn back and said, "You will be free or die." The Underground Railroad was big business. John Hope Franklin quotes Governor Quitman of Mississippi as saying that the South lost one hundred thousand slaves between 1810 and 1850. These "happy—satisfied" slaves risked their lives fleeing from slavery, fought for freedom, and used every device they knew to break the chains of slavery.

The work of the Abolitionists is another path the slaves traveled in their search for freedom. By far the most widely known Negro abolitionist was Frederick Douglass. He was brilliant, eloquent, and courageous. On September 2, 1838, Douglass escaped from slavery. He went to Philadelphia, then to New York, and later to

Massachusetts. He soon met the antislavery group, and traveled and preached for the Massachusetts Society. He came to know Garrison and Phillips Brooks. He traveled about the country speaking against slavery. He was eloquent in speech and attracted large crowds. Fearing that his popularity would lead to his being detected and enslaved again, with $250 raised by friends he sailed for England in August of 1845. He remained in England two years. Having become famous as an orator and abolitionist, he could have stayed in England, but his desire for freedom for his people forced him to return. From 1847 to the close of the Civil War, he spoke, wrote, and preached against slavery. His newspaper, *The North Star*, was a powerful weapon against the institution of slavery. Even after emancipation, Douglass continued until his death in 1895 to lift up his voice against injustices of every description.[2]

We will now discuss paths to freedom which the Negro has used since 1865. Here, as in the previous pages, we can only point out the methods used, but we cannot do an exhaustive job. The first method used by Negroes, to free themselves from crippling restrictions imposed upon them after federal troops were withdrawn from the South in 1877, was the manly and courageous work of Negroes in legislatures of some of the southern states. South Carolina, for example, held a Constitutional Convention in 1895. A move was on for the Disfranchisement of Negroes.

There were six Negroes in the South Carolina Legislature at the time. Thomas E. Miller and Robert Smalls sought to stem the tide of disfranchisement. They did their best to get through a proposal guaranteeing the right to register and vote not only for Negroes but for every person, White and Black, man and woman. The resolution lost. The one-hundred and thirty white representatives voted against the resolution and the six Negroes voted for it.

---

[2] Ibid

Many years before women were given the ballot, farsighted Negro legislators were advocating women's suffrage. This was a lost cause, but it does show how the struggle for freedom continued almost immediately after physical emancipation.

Negroes in Congress also did their bit to free themselves and the South from the inhuman curse of lynching. At the turn of the century, lynching was a respected and revered institution in the South. In 1900, one hundred and fifteen Negroes were lynched. On January 20, 1900, a Negro, George H. White, introduced in the House of Representatives the first bill aimed at making lynching a federal offense. The bill was defeated and until this day no law has been passed to make lynching a federal offense.

Negroes in the state legislatures were also advocating the establishment of a public school system.

The Negro was disfranchised in 1895 in South Carolina. Ben Tillman started the move when he was elected governor in 1890. Although in the Senate in 1895, he did his share in getting the Negro disfranchisement. Tillman accused Negroes of having done nothing to demonstrate their capacity in government. Thomas Miller replied by pointing out that Negroes were largely responsible for laws enacted to strengthen the finances of the state, the building of penal and charitable institutions and "greatest of all, for the establishment of the public school system." It is not true that Negro legislators were mainly ignorant and dishonest, not knowing what the score was. There were able Negroes in Congress and in the state legislatures. Some of them were very able and were prophetic in their efforts to advance the cause of freedom and democracy.

No Negro up until Booker T. Washington's time nor since has so deeply impressed the American mind as he did. White America, both North and South, believed that Washington had found the one sure road that would bring freedom to the Negro and solve the race problem. His Atlanta speech in 1895 made him famous not only in America but throughout Europe. Whereas white America almost unanimously accepted his leadership, there were divisions among Negroes. And yet, the vast majority of Negroes accepted Washington's leadership. It could hardly have been otherwise. White America had made Washington the spokesman for Negro America. Besides, Booker T. Washington was one of America's great men.

The Atlanta speech made Booker T. Washington famous mainly because he said what white America wanted to hear. He urged Negroes not to bother about politics and social equality, but to cast down their buckets where they were. It is clear that men like Booker T. Washington had profound faith in the South and believed that as the Negro proved his competence in agriculture, in domestic service, mechanics and other areas, he would be accorded the full rights of citizenship. Although in no way opposing higher education, he did lay greater emphasis upon training the hands to do the skilled work of the South. The Atlanta speech made Booker T. Washington famous primarily because he sanctioned the segregated pattern of life. In fact, if a Negro had advocated the abolition of segregation in 1895, he would hardly have lived to tell the story. It would be interesting if we could know in what way Booker T. Washington's Atlanta speech influenced the 1896 decision of the United States Supreme Court when it made segregation constitutional. The Ferguson versus Plessy Decision may have definitely been influenced by Booker T. Washington's Atlanta speech.

Several passages in the Atlanta speech deserve quoting. He urged the Negroes to cast down their buckets among the friendly white people of the South, and he admonished the Whites to cast down their buckets among the Negroes whom they could trust.

173

He told the Negroes to cast it down in agriculture, in mechanics, in commerce, in domestic science, and in the professions, and in this connection it is well to bear in mind that whatever other sins the South may be called to bear, when it comes to business, pure and simple, it is in the South that the Negro is given a man's chance in the commercial world and in nothing is this exposition more eloquent than in emphasizing this chance.[3]

Perhaps the most widely quoted passage by the white south follows:

> "In all things that are purely social, we can be as separate as the fingers, yet one as the hand in all things essential to mutual progress. . . The wisest among my race understand that the agitation of questions of social equality is the extremist folly, and that progress and the enjoyment of all the privileges that will come to us must be the result of severe and constant struggle rather than artificial forcing. . . . The opportunity to earn a dollar in a factory just now is worth infinitely more than the opportunity to spend a dollar in an opera house."[4]

This path to freedom was greatly modified by the leadership of W.E. DuBois and the National Association for the Advancement of Colored People (NAACP). In *The Souls of Black Folk*, DuBois said in 1903:

> "The problem of the Twentieth century is the problem of the color line—the relation of the darker to the lighter races of men in Asia and Africa, in America and the Islands of the Sea."

---

[3] Ibid.

[4] Ibid.

In July, 1905, fifty-nine Negroes met near Buffalo, New York, to lay down a platform in opposition to Booker T. Washington. They believed that he was too acquiescent in his racial views. This group met again August 16-19, 1906, at Harper's Ferry, West Virginia.

At this meeting they called themselves the Niagara Movement. The following quotation sums up the philosophy of the Niagara Movement:

> "We will not be satisfied to take one jot or tittle less than our full manhood rights. We claim for ourselves every single right that belongs to a freeborn American, political and social. And until we get the rights, we will not cease to protest and assail the ears of America. The battle we wage is not for ourselves but for all true Americans."

This sums up the philosophy of DuBois at one time and expresses in part the program of the NAACP, which moves on a much broader basis that the Niagara Movement. When the NAACP was organized in 1910, the aspiration of the Niagara Movement was absorbed into it. In brief, it is the purpose of the NAACP to abolish racial discrimination and segregation in every aspect (public) of American life. The NAACP must be given credit for the vast majority of civil rights won before the Supreme Court. The NAACP holds that the Negro can never be free as long as he is segregated and discriminated against because of race and color. It has achieved great success traveling the legal paths to freedom. The move to equalize salaries in public education, the entrance of Negroes into the State Universities of the South, the 1954 decision of the Supreme Court declaring segregation in the public schools unconstitutional, the abolition of segregation in interstate travel, the abolition of the white primary, the removal of the restrictive covenant in housing, and many other civil rights decisions are traceable to the work of the NAACP and the Legal Defense Fund.

In a way, the battle between DuBois and Booker T. Washington continues in the more militant program of the NAACP. Although the NAACP does not make its main work the sponsoring of sit-ins, it has participated in student demonstrations, encouraged the students, and defended them in court. The NAACP, up to now, has more to show for its civil rights activities than any other organization.

Another path to freedom utilized by Negroes is the National Urban League. It is an interracial organization, designed to free the Negro from the curse of low wages and his low economic status. The League believes that no group can be free without full participation in the economic and industrial life of America. Although interested in every phase of Negro life, the National Urban League concentrates on a program designed to upgrade Negroes in the places where they work and secure employment in places where Negroes have never worked. It has had huge success in finding new positions for Negroes, getting them upgraded, but always on the basis of merit. The League gets the facts and moves in on the basis of carefully documented evidence. It assumes that if Negroes are thoroughly competent, the doors of prejudice and discrimination must yield. It keeps contact with the leading industries of the country.

XXI

BLACK HERITAGE

I am amazed at what I see in terms of accomplishments of people of color. In spite of a system that was against us, the true record will reflect that black folks were not only cotton pickers, babysitters, "house Niggers," nervous nellies, scratching when they were not itching, and grinning when they were not tickled, but served their country with dignity and respect. Please read the record:

Inventors

Invention is not peculiar to man, but in degree is characteristic of man. Black inventions range from simple household conveniences to more complex mechanical devices, which have proved to be of vital importance to business and industry. Some are as familiar as. . .

—The potato chip of Hyram S. Thomas, a Saratoga chef
—The ice cream of Augustus Jackson, a Philadelphia confectioner (1832).

—The gold tee of George F. Grant.
—The mop holder of Thomas W. Stewart.
—The player pianos of J.H. and S.L. Dickinson.

Others are more complex, such as the lubricating machines of Elijah McCoy; electric street lighting of Louis H. Latimer, and the shoe-lasting (shaping) machine of Jan Ernst Matzeliger.

One of the first black inventors was James Forten, who invented a method of sewing sails. The first patent issued and recorded to a Black was to Henry Blair of Maryland, a free Black who obtained a patent for a corn harvester in 1834.

In 1831, Jo Anderson, a black slave, assisted Cyrus McCormick in creating the grain harvester.

Anthony Weston, in 1831, improved the threshing machine invented by W.T. Catto.

From 1872 until he died in 1910, Granville T. Woods invented many devices in the field of telegraphy, including telegraphing from moving trains.

Lewis Temple invented the toggle harpoon for whaling, which more than doubled the catch for this New England industry.

Horace King, born a slave, was one of the foremost bridge engineers in the south before the Civil War.

Thomas L. Jennings, a free Black, patented a device for renovating clothes.

Dr. Norval Cobb Vaughn invented and patented a bulletproof shield.

Norbert Rilleux, in 1846, invented and patented a vacuum pan.

The largest number of patents issued to a black inventor went to Elijah McCoy, who received his first patent in 1872 and his last—his fifty-seventh—in 1920. Most dealt with lubrication systems credited with perfecting the systems used in large industries today.

William B. Purvis designed his first machine for making paper bags in 1882.

Andrew J. Beard was granted a patent on an automatic car coupling device in 1897.

Frederick M. Jones developed the first practical refrigerator system for trucks and railroad freight cars.

Emmanuel M. Moore of Pine Bluff, Arkansas, designed an earth moving machine.

Henry Boyd invented a machine to produce rails for beds, but had to obtain a patent in the name of a white man.

Elbert R. Robertson invented the grooved wheel used by all railroads.

There were approximately three hundred and forty-one inventions patented by Blacks between 1834 and 1900, many of which are in use today. Among these are the following:

—Gas Inhalator, by Garrett A. Morgan
—First Clock in America, made by Benjamin Banneker
—Shampoo Headrest, by C. O. Bailiff, 1898
—Ironing Board, by Sarah Boone, 1892
—Lawn Mower, by J.A. Burr, 1899
—Range, by T.A. Carrington, 1876
—Cotton Chopper, by W.H. Richardson, 1886
—Oil Stove and Refrigerator, by J. Standard, 1889 and 1891.

*(In cases where an inventor has patented several variations on the same basic invention, a composite entry has been devised.)

Inventor	Invention	Date	Patent
Abrams, W.B.	Hame attachment	Apr. 14, 1891	450,550
Allen C.W.	Self-leveling table	Nov. 01, 1898	613,436
Allen J.B.	Clothesline support	Dec. 10, 1895	551,105
Ashbourne, A.P.	Process for preparing coconut for domestic use	June 01, 1875	163,962
	Biscuit cutter	Nov. 30, 1875	170,460
	Refining coconut oil	July 27, 1880	230,518
	Treating coconut process	Aug. 21, 1877	194,287
Baffles, William	Ladder scaffold support	Aug. 05, 1879	218,154
Bailey, L.C.	Combined Truss & bandage	Sept. 25, 1883	285,545
	Folding bed	July 18, 1899	629,286
Ballow, W.J.	Combined hatrack table	Mar. 29, 1898	601,422
Barnes, G.A.E.	Design for sign	Aug. 19, 1889	29,193
Beard, A.J.	Rotary engine	July 05, 1892	478,271
	Car-coupler	Nov. 23, 1897	594,059
Becket, G.E.	Letter box	Oct. 04, 1892	483,525
Bell, L.	Locomotive smokestack	May 23, 1871	115,153
	Dough kneader	Dec. 10, 1872	133,823
Benjamin, L.W.	Broom moisteners/bridles	May 16, 1893	497,747
Benjamin, Miss M.	Gong/signal chairs for hotels	July 17, 1888	386,286
Binga, M.W.	Street sprinkling apparatus	July 22, 1879	217,843
Blackburn, A.B.	Railway signal	Jan. 10, 1888	376,362
	Spring seat for chairs	Apr. 03, 1888	380,420
	Cash carrier	Oct. 23, 1888	391,577
Blair, Henry	Corn planter	Oct. 14, 1834	8447x
	Cotton planter	Aug. 31, 1836	Not #'d
Blue, L.	Hand corn shelling device	May 20, 1884	298.937
Booker, L.F.	Rubber scraping knife	Mar. 28, 1899	30,404
Bowman, H.A.	Making flags	Feb. 23, 1892	469,395
Brooks, C.B.	Punch	Oct. 31, 1893	507,672
	Street-sweepers	Mar. 17, 1896	556,711
	Street-sweepers	May 12, 1896	560,154
Brooks, Hallstead & Page	Street-sweepers	Apr. 21, 1896	558,719
Brown, Henry	Receptacle for storing and preserving papers	Nov. 02, 1886	352,036
Brown, L.F.	Bridle bit	Oct. 25, 1892	484,994
Brown, O.E.	Horse shoe	Aug. 23, 1892	481,271
Brown & Latimer	Water closets for railway cars	Feb. 10, 1874	147,363
Burr, J.A.	Lawn mower	May 09, 1899	624,749
Burr, W.F.	Switching device for railways	Oct. 31, 1899	636,197
Burwell, W.	Boot or shoe	Nov. 28, 1899	638,143
Butler, R.A.	Train alarm	June 15, 1897	584,540
Butts, J.W.	Luggage carrier	Oct. 10, 1899	634,611
Byrd, T.J.	Improvements in holders for reins for horses	Feb. 06, 1872	123,238

180

Inventor	Invention	Date	Patent
Byrd, T.J.	Apparatus for detaching horses from carriages	Feb. 06, 1872	123,238
	Apparatus for detaching horses from carriages	Mar. 19, 1872	124,79
Campbell, W.S.	Self-setting animal trap	Aug. 30, 1881	246,369
Cargill, B.F.	Invalid cot	July 25, 1899	639,658
Carrington, T.A.	Range	July 25, 1899	180,323
Carter, W.C.	Umbrella stand	Aug. 04, 1085	323,397
Certain, J.M.	Parcel Carrier for bicycles	Dec. 26, 1899	639,708
Cherry, M.A.	Velocipede	May 08, 1888	383,397
	Street car fender	Jan. 01, 1895	531,908
Church, T.S.	Carpet beating machine	July 29, 1884	302,237
Clare, O.B.	Trestle	Oct. 09, 1888	390,752
Coates, R.	Overboot for horses	Apr. 19, 1892	473,295
Cook, G.	Automatic Fishing device	May 30, 1899	625,829
Coolidge, J.S.	Harness attachment	Nov. 13, 1888	392,908
Cooper, J.	Shutter and fastening	May 01, 1883	276,563
	Elevator device	Apr. 02, 1895	536,605
	Elevator device	Sept. 21, 1897	590,257
Cornwell, P.W.	Draft regulator	Oct. 02, 1888	390,284
	Draft regulator	Feb. 07, 1893	491,082
Cralle, A.L.	Ice cream mold	Feb. 02, 1897	576,395
Creamer, H.	Steam feed water trap	Mar. 17, 1895	313,854
	Steam trap feeder	Dec. 11, 1888	394,463
Cosgrove, W.F.	Gas oil pipe automatic stop plugs	Mar. 17, 1885	313,993
Darkins, J.T.	Ventilation aid	Feb. 19, 1895	534,322
Davis, I.D.	Tonic	Nov. 02, 1886	351,829
Davis, W.D.	Riding saddles	Oct. 06, 1896	568,939
Davis, W.R. Jr	Library table	Sept. 24, 1878	208,278
Deitz, W.A.	Shoe	Apr. 30, 1867	64,205
Dickinson, J.H.	Pianola	Michigan 1899	
Dorsey, O.	Door-holding device	Dec. 10, 1878	10,764
Dorticus, C.J.	Device for applying coloring liquids to sides of soles or heels of shoes	Mar. 19, 1895	535,82
Dorticus, C.J.	Embossing photo machine	Apr. 16, 1895	537,442
	Photographic print wash	Apr. 23, 1875	537,968
	Hose leak stop	July 18, 1899	629,315
Downing, P.B.	Electric switch for railroad	June 17, 1890	430,118
	Letter box	Oct. 27, 1891	462,093
	Street letter box	Oct. 27, 1891	462,096
Dunnington, T.H.	Horse detachers	Mar. 16, 1897	578,979
Edmonds, T.H.	Separating screens	July 20, 1897	586,724
Elkins, T.	Dining, ironing table & quilting frame combined	Feb. 22, 1870	100,020
	Chamber commode	Jan. 09, 1872	122,518
	Refrigerator apparatus	Nov. 04, 1879	221,222

181

Inventor	Invention	Date	Patent
Evans, J.H.	Convertible setters	Oct. 05, 1897	591,095
Faulkner, H.	Ventilated shoes	Apr. 29, 1890	426.495
Ferrell, F.J.	Steam trap	Feb. 11, 1890	420,993
	Snow melting apparatus	May 27, 1890	428,670
	Valve	May 27, 1890	428,671
Fisher, D.A.	Joiners' clamp	Apr. 20, 1875	162,281
Flemmings, F. Jr	Guitar	Mar. 30, 1886	338,727
Latimer & Tregoning	Electric lamp globe support	Mar. 21, 1882	255,212
Lavalette, W.	Printing press	Sept. 17, 1878	208,208
Lee, H.	Animal trap	Feb. 12, 1867	61,941
Lee, J.	Kneading machine	Aug. 07, 1894	524,042
	Bread crumbing machine	June 04, 1895	540,553
Leslie, F.W.	Envelope seal	Sept. 21, 1897	590,325
Lewis, A.L.	Window cleaner	Sept. 27, 1892	483,359
Lewis, E.R.	Spring gun	May 03, 1887	362,096
Linden, H.	Piano truck	Sept. 08, 1891	459,365
Little, E.	Bridle bit	March 07, 1882	254,666
Loudin, F.J.	Sash fastener	Dec. 12, 1892	510,432
	Key fastener	Jan. 09, 1894	512,308
Love, J.L.	Plasterer's hawk	July 09, 1895	542,419
	Pencil sharpener	Nov. 23, 1897	594,114
Marshall, T.J.	Fire extinguisher	May 26, 1872	125,063
Marshall, W.	Grain binder	May 11, 1886	341,599
Martin, W.A.	Lock	July 23, 1890	407,738
	Lock	Dec. 30, 1890	443,945

War Heroes

The Revolutionary War (1775-1781)

Crispus Attucks was one of the first martyrs to American Independence. Every major battle during the war included Negroes in its troops. Peter Salem and Salem Poor were singled out for gallantry.

The War of 1812

Three Negro seamen were aboard the British ship when the Chesapeake Incident signaled the start of the War of 1812. By the end of the war, one of every six members of the Navy was a Black. William Brown was cited for courage and service.

The Battle of New Orleans (1815)

An integrated army, including two Negro battalions, defeated British troops.

The Civil War (1861-1865)

The Negro soldier fought bravely and won praise in more than two hundred battles. Twenty won the Medal of Honor, America's highest military honor.

The Indian Fighters

Negro units of the Army helped keep the uneasy peace in the Western territories. Fourteen Negroes won the Congressional Medal of Honor.

The Spanish American War

Four black units were sent to Cuba under America's highest ranking black officer, Major Charles Young. All four earned the Medal of Honor.

World War I

There were 404,348 Negro troops. Henry Johnson and Needham Young of the 93rd Infantry, 369th Regiment, became the first Americans of any race to earn the French Croix de Guerre.

World War II

Dorie Miller was America's first hero on December 7, 1941, when he shot down six Zeros with a machine gun, which he had never fired before. He was awarded the Navy Cross. More than a million Blacks entered the armed forces. Seven thousand served as officers; four commanded Merchant Marine ships; Colonel Benjamin O. Davis flew sixty missions.

Korea

The policy of complete integration in the United States Army was adopted in January, 1950. The first to integrate was the eighty-one-year-old, all-black, 24th Infantry. Two black soldiers were award the Congressional Medal of Honor.

Vietnam

By 1965, according to Defense Department figures, almost 15 percent of the Navy, 8.9 percent of the Marine Corps, and 8.3 percent of the Air Force were Blacks. Nineteen were awarded the Congressional Medal of Honor. Fifty-nine Blacks had been awarded the Congressional Medal of Honor by 1969. In addition, the Navy Medal of Honor had been awarded to nine others.

How Blacks Excelled in Music

The music of black people has always been, and remains, a key force behind events: the civil rights movement could not have evolved as it did without the songs of the freedom marchers. Recent discoveries of excellent black symphonic music, both contemporary and two centuries old, prove that black music has always been more than a limited program of spiritual, jazz and blues. Joseph Haydn, Beethoven's teacher, is also described by his biographers as "a moor" (the word used to describe the Negro in all the countries of the Western world). George P. Bridgetower, Polish-born son of an African, took Paris by storm in 1879 with his first major violin concert at the age of ten. Also composer Bridgetower was recommended by Beethoven "for further exposure." In a period as early as 1840-1876, the work and talent of black musicians and singers commanded the attention of the white press. Eugene V. McCarty of New Orleans, in 1840, studied voice, harmony and composition at the Imperial Conservatory of Paris. In the 1840's, Sarah Sedgewick Bowers sang operatic arias in Philadelphia and New York. Elizabeth Taylor Greenfield, "The Black Swan," sang at Buckingham Palace in 1854 at the invitation of Queen Victoria. Cleveland Luca migrated to Liberia about 1860 and composed the National Anthem of that country. Edwin Hill was the first Negro to be admitted to the Philadelphia Academy of Fine Arts (1871). Basile Bares, New Orleans-born pianist and composer, toured France in 1867. Flora Batson, born in 1870, toured the United States, Europe, Australia, and New Zealand as a concert ballad singer. Mrs. Sampson Williams, a soprano, made a successful tour of Europe in 1800 using the professional name of "Mme. Marie Selika." In 1871, "The Colored Opera Company" presented outstanding works under John Esputa. The Boston Musical Union was formed in 1875 and 1876, and Blacks organized the New York Philharmonic Society. The Samuel Coleridge Taylor Musical Society of Washington boasted over two hundred black members in 1903.

Composers and Arrangers

Harry T. Burleigh, singer, composer, arranger (1866-1949), toured the concert halls of the United States and Europe and was twice honored with performances for King Edward, VII. Burleigh was arranging spirituals for the concert stage at the turn of the century. Nathaniel Dett (1882-1943), made significant contributions to America's musical heritage with his compositions and arrangements. His opera "The Ordering of Moses" was performed in the forties by the National Negro Company and presented at Carnegie Hall in 1951. W.C. Handy, musician and composer (1873-1958), in addition to being acclaimed "The Father of The Blues," was also a choral and orchestra conductor performing at Carnegie Hall in 1928 in a musical history of the Negro. He wrote "Afro-American Hymn: Blue Destiny," a symphonic piece, and over 150 compositions, both sacred and secular. James Bland (1854-1911) composed Southern songs (folk songs). Dr. James Weldon Johnson was a musicologist, journalist, poet, and educator. He and his brother, J. Rosamong Johnson, wrote "Under the Bamboo Tree," a popular hit, which enjoyed radio and TV exposure for over sixty years.

Conductors

Dean Dixon, at age twenty-six, became the first Black to ever conduct the New York Philharmonic Orchestra. A few other conductors of note were: William Levi Dawson, composer- conductor, noted for "I Couldn't Hear Nobody Pray"; James DePriest, conductor, William Grant Still, modern composer, who conducted the Los Angeles Philharmonic Orchestra in 1936, a long way from his Woodville, Mississippi home and the "honkey -tonk" dives of the deep South. Ulysses Kay (1917) ranks high among serious black composers.

Concert Artists

The list of concert artists is too long to name, but here are a few of the most outstanding: Roland Hayes, Paul Robeson, Marian Anderson, and Etta Moten Barnett carried vocal music to new heights of technical finesse. Also Martina Arroyo, Lillian Evanti, Todd Duncan, Dorothy Maynor, Carol Brice, Mattiwilda Dobbs, Robert McFerrin, Leontyne Price, William Warfield, Grace Bumbry, and other artists have continued the fine tradition for superb singing in concerts, folk opera and grand opera. Concert pianists include: Louis Mareau Gottschalk, composer-pianist (1820), probably the first black composer born in the U.S. to achieve international renown; Phillippa Schuyler (1932-1969); George Walker (1922-   ); and Andre Watts, one of America's most gifted pianists.

The Negro Spiritual

From their experiences as slaves, Blacks developed the spirituals, which rank among the classical folk expressions because of their moving simplicity, characteristic originality, and universal appeal. In his essay "Of the Sorrow Songs," W.E.B. DuBoise called the spirituals the "music of an unhappy people. . ." The spirituals were first noted during the abolitionist period, but soon died away until the Fisk Jubilee Singers took them before the world in the 1870's. They are now immortal. J. Rosamond Johnson, Harry T. Burleigh, Carl Diton, Nathaniel Dett, and John R. Work are among the most renowned composers and arrangers. Secular music derived from the spirituals. Through his music, the Afro-

187

American has opened one door to fame and fortune by himself. . . the wonderful world of music. His repertoire is unlimited; he has covered all portals: Classical and operatic, folk, spirituals, ragtime, jazz, blues, rock, disco—the works. And through it all, he has left his mark.

Performing Arts

The Negro has made a truly enormous contribution to the world of American entertainment. The vitality of his influence on American music, dance and drama has been irresistible—its impact profound and lasting. Before slavery ended, the Negro had started to permeate popular music and eventually dominated it. Negro slaves provided the music of the plantations both for themselves and for the white owners. Starting as a figure of ridicule, a comic type and object of the white man's amusement, he has slowly moved to a position of dignity and even protest and struggle. He acquired professional polish and finally emerged as a creative performer of more than one dimension.

Drama

Shakespeare's "Othello" was a black man, followed in 1696 by "Oroonoko," whose hero was an African prince. Both roles were played on stage by Blacks. Free Blacks in New York City formed the "African Company" in 1821, and placed black actors in the history books. James Hewlett, the leading member, specialized in the roles of Othello and Richard III. About this same period, Ira Aldridge (1807-1867), appeared and vitalized acting and actors. Blacks were first cast in white productions about 1877. A black Topsy appeared in "Uncle Tom's Cabin" in 1897. "The Creole Show" in 1891 glamorized the black girl for the first time. "The

Octoroon"(1895) and "Oriental America" (1896) are other landmarks in the emergence of Blacks in the theater. Bert Williams, Bob Cole and Will-Marion Cook gained theatrical prominence.

Appearing about 1920 were: Charles Gilpin in O'Neil's "The Emperor Jones;" Paul Robeson, "All of God's Chillun;" Noble Sissie and Eubie Blake produced "Shuffle Along;" "Porgy" appeared on stage, and Josephine Baker, Florence Mills, Richard Mills, and Richard B. Harrison gained attention. (Harrison: "De Lawd"). The next twenty-five years saw many notable productions and stars. A few were: "Anna Lucasta," "Native Son," Loraine Hansberry's "Raisin In The Sun," and Lillia Smith's "Strange Fruit," pushing toward stardom Hilda Simms, Canada Lee, Sidney Poitier and Claudia McNeil. Black actors have won Oscars, Tonies, Emmies, and other awards.

Mass Entertainment

A notable number of Blacks have become household names in mass entertainment. At the end of 1968, more than fourteen television shows featured Blacks in major roles. The number has vastly increased. Behind the cameras, Robert Goodwin produced scripts for such shows as "Judd for the Defense," "The Big Valley," and "Julia." Mal Goode became one of the first black newscasters when he faced the cameras for ABC in the late '60's. He has been followed by hundreds on all major national networks and on local programming. In all of the performing and informing arts, Blacks have debated their roles: Could they write, act, sing, or report independent of their status as black men and women? The answer has been an emphatic "yes." Blacks have inscribed their names on a wide spectrum of talent ranging from concert to theater to variety stage to mass media. Sidney Poitier has been described as a "superstar." Jim

Brown discarded a football to "light up" Hollywood. Raymond St. Jaques, Percy Rodriques, Brock Peters, Diana Ross, Lena Horne, Hattie McDaniel, and scores of others will be remembered for outstanding performances in feature films.

Blacks Pioneered in Medicine

The Negro people brought with them from Africa a medicine not much different from the "kitchen physick" flourishing in Colonial America. They had their medicine men and conjure women, but they also had their own "materia medica," the product of centuries of practical experience. They knew the medicinal value of a wide assortment of mineral, plant, and herb mixes, with the result that "root doctoring" occupied a prominent place in the therapeutic arsenal of many southern plantations. They even knew of the practice of "buying the smallpox." The white minister credited with introducing this practice into colonies in the early Eighteenth Century learned of it from a Negro slave. Negro midwives brought medical knowledge from Africa concerning birth by Cesarean section. With such a background, Negro slaves took to the healing arts. As early as 1740, a fugitive slave was described as "being able to bleed and draw teeth."

In 1751, a Negro named Cesar discovered a cure for rattlesnake bite. Another slave-born Negro, David K. McDonough, was licensed to practice medicine and served on the staff of New York's Eye and Ear Infirmary. The first private hospital for Negroes in New York was named in his honor.

Santomee, a slave, was trained in Holland and studied medicine among the Dutch and English in New York. Another slave, Oneissimus, developed an antidote for smallpox in 1721. Other early black physicians, most of whom were self-taught, included James Still (1810), David Ruggles (1810), and William Wells

Brown (1816), all well-known, also, as abolitionists. James Derham is generally regarded as the first trained black physician. During the 1780's, he became one of the most prominent physicians in New Orleans. Dr. John S. Rock practiced medicine and dentistry for eleven years before being sworn in as the first Negro to argue cases of law before the Supreme Court. Martin Delaney was trained in medicine at Harvard (1852). Eight black licensed physicians served with a regiment. Assigned to Washington hospitals were C.B. Purvis, A. Tucker, William Powell, John Rapier, William Ellis, A.R. Abbott, and A.T. Augusta.

Howard University's School of Medicine and Meharry Medical College were established in 1876. Beginning in 1882, six others were founded, but disappeared during the early 20th Century. At the turn of the century, the "Big Four" of Negro physicians were Dr. Daniel Hale Williams; Dr. George Cleveland Hall, Chicago surgeon and diagnostician; Dr. Auston M. Curtis, Chicago protege of Dr. Williams; and Dr. Nathan F. Mossell, founder of the Frederick Douglass Hospital in Philadelphia. Dr. Daniel Hale Williams made history with the first successful open heart operation.

From World War I to World War II, all Negro medical personnel continued to fight against great odds. But in spite of these difficulties, a number made striking contributions to the progress of American medicine and science. Among these were: Dr. Louis T. Wright, antibiotic Aureomycin; Dr. William A. Hinton, the Hinton Test for syphilis; Dr. T.K. Lawless, noted dermatologist; Dr. Jane Cook Wright-Jones, cancer chemotherapy; Dr. Ulysses Grant Dailey, founder-fellow International College of Surgeons; Dr. Charles Drew, blood plasma; and Dr. W. Montague Cobb, anatomist at Howard University. These and many others were fighting against the postscript of Dr. W.E.B. DuBois: *"Our death rate is without a doubt. . . due to poverty and discrimination."*

191

Athletics and Sports

Sports is an area in which the black man's preeminence has already captured world-wide attention. Amateur and professional athletes have reached stardom in virtually all the major sports engaged in by Americans and, in so doing, have created vast audiences of dedicated fans both at home and abroad.

Baseball

In the years since Jackie Robinson broke the color barrier in major league baseball, black stars have become too numerous to name. But, before then Andrew "Rube" Foster, in (1905) reportedly pitched fifty-one victories in fifty-five exhibition games against white major and minor leagues. Josh Gibson played professional baseball from the 1920's to the 1940's. In 1971, his name was added to Baseball's Hall of Fame. Satchell Paige became a baseball legend. Hank Aaron belted the 715th home run of his career on April 8, 1974, breaking Babe Ruth's long-standing record.

Many of the early stars of the game played out their careers before 1969. This applies to such stalwart players as Dan Bankhead and Joe Black, Brooklyn Dodger pitchers; Monty Irvin and Hank Thompson, New York Giants; Sam Jethroe, Boston Braves; Luke Easter and Harry "Suitcase" Simpson, Cleveland Indians, and a number of others. There is hardly a single position in the game at which at least one black star has not excelled as: pitcher—Don Newcombe, catchers—Roy Campanella and Elston Howard; infielder—Maury Willis; outfielder—Willie Mays. Year after year, black players continue to earn high standings in both Leagues in all areas of the game. More recent black baseball stars include Barry Bonds, Ken Griffey Jr., Tony Gynn, Ricky

Henderson, Reggie Jackson, David Justice, Kirby Puckett, Hilton Smith, and Dave Winfield.

Football

Black men were prominent in professional football from 1919 to 1933. Thereafter, they disappeared until 1946, when the L.A. Rams signed Kenny Washington and Woody Strode, and the Cleveland Browns signed Bill Willis and Marion Motle. Jim Brown rewrote most of the professional record book, but he is only one of several black stars who have dominated the game.

In the era before 1946, Fritz Pollard and Joe Lillard made outstanding records. The premier black performers emerged in the late fifties and early sixties, including such players as Lenny Moore, Jim Parker, and Dick "Night Train" Lane. The late sixties saw the emergence of black performers at positions that had traditionally been restricted to white ballplayers. Since then, the numbers have continued to grow, and the performances have continued to excel. The last position to give way to a Black was quarterback, but eventually that, too, came. Today, as the kickoff is made, black stars cover all offensive and defensive positions on the field, in addition to calling the plays. Among the greatest football players of all times are Jim Brown, Tony Dorsett, Key Shawn Johnson, Ray Lewis, Steve McNair, Warren Moon, Walter Payton, Eddie Robinson, Barry Sander, Deion Sanders, Jackie Slater, Lynn Swann, and Doug Williams.

Basketball

The first black man to play professional basketball in the NBA was Chuck Cooper, signed by the Boston Celtics in 1950. Since then many of the top players in both Leagues have been black men. However, as in other fields, black players have historically broken records on segregated courts as early as 1923, when the New York Rens were organized by Robert J. Douglas, one of the earliest pro teams of any race. The Harlem Globetrotters were organized in 1927. By 1960, many of the top players in both leagues were black men, among whom were Bill Russell, K.C. Jones and Elgin Baylor.

The late 1960's saw many new and highly talented black ballplayers. Heading this list was probably Lew Alcindor (Kareem Abdull Jabaar). Many other players have made outstanding records, such as Elvin Hayes, Wes Unseld, Walt Frazier, and Willis Reed. Since them, the numbers have continued to increase, with some of those early players retiring to other positions both on the courts and administratively. Most basketball experts agree that at least four black men belong with the greatest players yet produced in the field: Wilt Chamberlain, Bill Russell, Elgin Baylor, Oscar Robertson, Charles Barkley, Kobe Bryant, Marcus Camby, Vince Carter, John Choney, Sean Elliott, Kelvin Garnett, Horace Grant, A.C. Green, Yolanda Griffith, Grant Hill, Chamique Holdsclaw, Juwan Howard, Larry Hughes, Allen Iverson, Dr. J, Magic Johnson, Shawn Kemp, Lisa Leslie, Moses Malone, Tracey McGrady, Alonzo Mourning, Shaquille O'Neal, Amos Odom, John Salley, Isaiah Thomas, and Chris Webber.

Boxing

The Negro prizefighter has been active in America for well over two centuries. In fact, the first American heavyweight contender was a Black, Tom Molineaux, a Virginia slave. Jack Johnson won the heavyweight championship of the world, the first and only fighter to hold three titles at once. Joe Louis took the heavyweight crown in 1937. Since then, for all but about five years, a black man has held the heavyweight championship of the world. It was Sugar Ray Robinson, however, who has been acclaimed by experts as the most skillful pound-for-pound fighter who has ever lived.

Other greats include Muhammad Ali, George Foreman, Joe Frasier, Evander Holyfield, Roy Jones, Satchel Paige, and Mike Tyson.

Track and Field

The number of black stars in track and field include such World, Olympic, and American recordholders as Jesse Owens, who won four gold medals at the Olympic games in Berlin in 1936; Ralph Metcalfe, recognized Olympic star; Wilma Rudolph—three gold medals in 1960, and Rafer Johnson, who set a Decathlon Olympic record in Rome in 1960. Less widely recognized, however, have been such stars as George C. Poag, third place in the two hundred and four hundred meter hurdles, 1904; Dehart Hubbard, first place in running broad jump, 1924, and Eddie Tolan, Olympic and World record, 1932. More recently, Marion Jones, Jackie Joyner-Kirksey, and Wilma Rudolph have excelled. These are but a few of the Blacks who have made history performing under the American flag.

Golf

Charlie Sifford was the first black golfer to win admission to the PGA. In the late 1960's, Lee Elder and Pete Brown joined the circuit. Professional golf also has Ethel Funches, a top black woman golfer on the circuit. And of course, what needs to be said about Tiger Woods?

Tennis

Although Blacks have rarely competed in tennis over the years, the indomitable Arthur Ash was one exception. A champion at the game, he may well have been a role model for the likes of Althen Gibson, Serena Williams and her sister Venus Williams.

Soccer

Soccer, like tennis, has not traditionally included Blacks among its players—but a few have been outstanding. They include, Jamar and DaMarcus Beasley, Tim Howard, Edward Johnson, Cobi Jones, and Eddie Pope.

Others

Isaac Murphy was the first jockey to win three Kentucky Derbies (1891). Tennis has Arthur Ashe and Althea Gibson, among others. Relatively few Blacks have set records in wrestling, swimming, hockey, and bowling, but these sports are not without black participation.

Civil Rights

Some early significant documents in American History, which bear a special relevance to the context of Black History in the United States are as follows:

The Germantown Mennonite Resolution
Against slavery (1688):
This represents the earliest such protest formally voiced in Colonial America. It was passed sixty-nine years after the introduction of the first Negro slaves in America.

The Declaration of Independence (1776):
The final version, as accepted by Congress, did not contain a paragraph written by Thomas Jefferson from which the following excerpt is taken: "He has waged cruel war against

human nature, violating its most sacred rights of life and liberty in the persons of a distant people who never offended him, captivating and carrying them into slavery in another hemisphere, or to incur miserable death in their transportation thither. . . ."

The Constitution of the United States (1787):
It contains passages attesting to the conservatism existing in the U.S. and provides for extension of slavery for a twenty-year period, and contains the so-called "three-fifths compromise."

The Bill of Rights (1791):
It was intended to protect certain rights of the people.

George Washington's Last Will and Testament:
The First President frees his slaves (1799), and reflects concern for the financial welfare and education of his former slaves.

Act to Prohibit the Importation of Slaves (1807).

The Missouri Compromise (1819-1921).

Inaugural Edition of *Freedom's Journal*:
The first Negro newspaper in the U.S.A. (1827):
It was owned and edited by Samuel Cornish and John B. Russwurm.

The Liberator: Most Famous Abolitionist
Newspaper in the United States (1831):
It's founder, William Lloyd Garrison, was White.

The North Star:
The Abolitionist Organ of Frederick Douglass Independence Day Address (1852).

The Kansas-Nebraska Act (1854):

It repealed the Missouri Compromise, giving the territories the right to decide if they would be slave or free territories.

Emancipation Proclamation (1863):
The Freedmen's Bureau (1865):

It was designed to provide basic health and educational services for freedmen.

The Thirteenth Amendment (1865):

Abolishes slavery.

The Civil Rights Act (1866):

It was designed to protect freedmen from The Black Codes and other repressive legislation.

The Fourteenth Amendment (1868):

Defined United States citizenship.

The Fifteenth Amendment (1870):

Established the right to vote.

The Civil Rights Act (1875):

Prohibits racial discrimination in public accommodation.

Booker T. Washington's
"Atlanta Compromise Speech" (1895):

Controversial.

The Universal Negro Improvement Association
Speech, New York City (1922):

By Marcus Garvey, the precursor of the present day Negro Nationalist Movement.

The Civil Rights Acts of 1957 and 1960:
First comprehensive federal civil rights legislation in the Twentieth Century.

Letter from a Birmingham Jail (1963):
This letter with the Birmingham Manifesto (1963) herald Martin Luther King's legacy to black Americans.

The Civil Rights Act of 1964:
And subsequent acts, manifestos, and executive orders, expanded legislation and concerns for the rights of all Americans.

Science & Industry

In 1870, more than 80 percent of the Negroes in the United States were illiterate and, even forty years later, more than one-third of the black population over ten years of age had still never been to school. It is against this background of systematic educational deprivation that the achievements of the Negro's development in science and industry can be seen in their sharpest perspective. The Negro scientist also encountered many legal and social obstacles. Innumerable scientific contributions which promoted industrial development never reached the history books.

The principal occupation of Negroes, as listed in the 1910 Census, was agricultural. Of the industrial occupations, skilled trades were represented by some thousands of black workers and included any and all occupations. Their employment, in fact, led to many inventions, which improved the American way of life. Statistics show that in 1850, free Negro males were engaged as architects, barbers, blacksmiths, boatmen, book binders, brick masons, brokers, cabinet makers, carpenters, clothiers, engineers, gunsmiths, merchants, shoemakers, and many others. The majority, however, were engaged in agricultural occupations—some 87.4 percent of the males and 54.7 percent of the females, which made this nation the vast agricultural Mecca for which it became known.

Black Americans have made significant contributions to science. Wilcie Elfce, of Charleston, South Carolina, was mixing prescriptions as early as 1853. One of the most diligent researchers was Dr. Charles Turner of St. Louis, who wrote at least forty-seven papers in the field of biology.

George Washington Carver founded a new branch of chemistry, called "chemurgy," defined as "the chemistry of the industrial use of organic raw materials," or "the industrial use of living things." From his Tuskegee Institute Laboratory in Alabama, he revolutionized southern agriculture. He used such raw material as peanuts, sweet potatoes, soy beans, and red clay to produce bleach, shampoo, flour, oil, coffee, and house paint, among others.

Norbert Rillieux revolutionized the sugar industry; James Cune Smith, a graduate of the University of Glasgow, Scotland, wrote scientific papers attacking the idea of racial inferiority; Lewis H. Latimer made important applications to the principal of electricity; and wrote the first text book on the Edison Electric System.

The list of black outstanding scientists include such men as J. Ernest Wilkins, who earned a Ph.D. in mathematics at age nineteen; Dr. Percy Julian, research chemist whose work in sterols has done much to improve the medical treatment of arthritis and glaucoma; Dr. Earnest E. Just, pure scientist, recognized for his work in the study of cells; and Dr. Merideth Gourdine, of Gourdine Industries, who organized a company which conducts research and produces equipment in electro-gas dynamics. Black scientists continue to make significant contributions through such pure and applied laboratories as Abbot Laboratories, Hoffman-Laroche, Baxter Laboratories, Douglas Aircraft, and biological and related institutions, including health and education. The black scientists—always considered exceptional—have given much—and continue to give—to the industrial and chemical development of this nation through their scientific studies, discoveries and pursuits.

Literature

Negro literature in America has been inextricably linked with the complex racial realities that have surrounded the black writer. With few exceptions, the major literary efforts of the American Negro have stemmed—directly or indirectly—from the existential facts of life for the black man in "white America." In the United States, Briton Hammon was the first black prose writer of record with "A Narrative . . . of Briton Hammon, A Negro Man" in 1760. The first poet was Lucy Terry with "Bars Flight" in 1746. One of the most prolific poets of the Eighteenth Century was Jupiter Hammon, a slave. Phillis Wheatley published her first poem in 1770. An important body of literature in black America is very recent. In centuries past, however, notable contributions were made to the literature from the Negroes' respective culture. Jacques Captein in Holland; Juan Latino in Spain; Alexander Pushkin in Russia, and Alexandre Dumas in France were writers of color whose skill placed them in the history books. The American writers and works mentioned here have been selected for their historical and or aesthetic importance. The list can only be minimally representative, but it serves as a tribute to American Negro writers and to the literary experience.

The birth of a real Negro literary tradition dates from 1853 when William Wells Brown wrote *Clotel*, a story of the hardships of a mulatto family. Charles Waddell Chestnut was the first to give serious consideration to the artistic requirements of the short story and novel. His works were published as early as 1887. W.E.B. DuBoise and James Weldon Johnson commanded national audiences when DuBoise wrote *Souls of Black Folks* in 1903, and Johnson produced his *Autobiography of an Ex-Coloured Man* in 1912. Countee Cullen carried poetry to new heights; Langston Hughes commanded attention and became known as the most durable of the Negro Renaissance. Hughes opened the thirties with *Not Without Laughter*. George Schuyler wrote *Black No More*, and the prolific Arna Bontemps published *God Sends Sunday*. Jesse Redmond Fauset appeared as probably the leading woman author of the Renaissance. The period also produced George W. Lee, Waters Turpin, George Henderson, William Attaway, and Zora Neale Hurston, prolific author of *Jonah's Gourd Vine*. Gwendolyn Brooks was winning a following.

Richard Wright's *Native Son* is often considered the beginning of the present stage in the evolution of the Negro literary tradition. He reached hundreds of thousands of readers of all races both in America and abroad. Willard Motley, with *Knock on Any Door*, Chester Himes with *If He Hollers, Let Him Go*, and Ann Petry's *The Street* preceded Ralph Ellison, who received the National Book Award in 1952 for *Invisible Man*.

A year later James Baldwin wrote *Go Tell it on the Mountain*. In the sixties, the number of black novelists increased enormously. Among the notables were: John O. Killen, Margaret Walker Alexander, Robert Dean Pharr, and William Melvin Kelly. Gwendolyn Brooks continued to be heard (in poetry), and Eldridge Cleaver was acclaimed a powerful essayist with his "Soul on Ice." While the current crop of young writers is promising, thus far nothing has come near to Alex Haley's *Roots*, and it is unlikely that anything will for a long time in the future.

Education

The African-American has long possessed a deep faith in the power of education to bring about a change in his status and in the conditions affecting his personal life. He has believed that education is the key to many of the shackles that bind him. In the days of slavery, this belief was strengthened by slave masters who, believing in the importance of education, declared it criminal for Blacks to learn to read and write.

The history of education for black Americans can be traced to the church. The Quakers in Philadelphia provided schools for Africans as early as 1774. In New York, The African Free School was opened in 1787. Primus Hall opened a school in his Boston home in 1798. General support for the education of free Blacks began in New Jersey in 1777.

Many Africans imported to the English colonies in 1619 had a brilliant cultural and educational background. As the importation of slaves increased, education in America met with great difficulties.

Statutes prohibiting education for Blacks were strengthened following the slave uprising by Nat Turner and Denmark Vesey, yet progress was made.

As early as 1787, Prince Hall petitioned the city of Boston to establish a school for black children. Societies and organizations devoted to the cause of education for Blacks date back to 1790. A few individual schools were established by churches, slaveholders and free Negroes. Yet, only two Negro institutions of higher learning existed prior to the Civil War: Wilberforce University (1856) and Lincoln University (1854). Immediately following the war, the Freedmen's Bureau established 4,239 schools with 9,307 teachers and 247,333 students. Ten colleges and universities were founded in the South between 1865 and 1876. Alcorn College became the first land-grant college to be started (1871). The next decade saw "agricultural and manual arts" or "agricultural and industrial" (A&M/A&I) colleges develop in nearly all of the ex-confederate states. The most celebrated, Tuskegee Institute (1881), is today a leading institution.

Probably the next major push in black education came with the Supreme Court decision of 1954, the implementation of which is of major concern today. Arriving at that momentous decision took the work, struggles and leadership of many men and women whose names are immortal. As a result of their efforts, the percentage of Blacks who have completed four of more years of college has been rising slowly and steadily. The list is too long to enumerate but is represented by such scholars as John Hope (1868-1936), educator, founder and President Atlanta University System; Macon B. Allen, first in the legal profession—the Dred Scott Case (1857) stemmed from his efforts to obtain a license to practice law; Edward A. Bouchet, first black Ph.D. (Yale, 1876, in physics); Booker T. Washington (1856-1915), whose name is almost synonymous with Tuskegee Institute; Laurence C. Jones, founder of Piney Woods Country Life School in 1909; John Hope Franklin (b. 1915); historian, educator, writer, and a Ph.D. from Harvard; W.E.B. DuBois (1868-1963), scholar, prophetic historian and writer; Arthur Schomburg (1874-1938), who established the Schomburg Collection as a living rebuttal to a teacher who said that the black man had no significant history; Carter G. Woodson (1875-1950), who organized the Association for the Study of Negro Life and History; Charlotte L. Forten Grimke

(1838-1914), abolitionist and teacher, and Elizabeth Evelyn Wright, who founded Voorhees College, 1894.

The major resource for training Negroes at the college level has long been the predominately black colleges and universities, most of which are located in the South. Public Negro colleges have existed for more than a century. Most were founded in the decades following the Civil War, between 1867 and 1900, to provide an education for newly freed slaves. The colleges are located in nineteen states. The oldest is Cheyney State College in Pennsylvania founded in 1837, and the only one predating the Civil War. The youngest is Mississippi Valley State, founded in 1950. Sixteen of the colleges were founded in the Nineteenth Century as land-grant schools. A majority were founded as state colleges, often with significant black leadership. Thirteen were initially organized under private auspices. The soldiers and officers of the 62nd United States Colored Infantry gave $5,000 to establish Lincoln University in Missouri. Financial problems led some private colleges to seek state supports and they became public institutions. There are now about seventy private black colleges.

What's Our Next Move?

It should be emphasized that an all-black society is not the answer to our social and political problems. The motto of the A.M.E. church is: "God our Father, Christ our Redeemer, and Man our Brother." Even if separation were psychologically sensible, which it is not, it does not make political sense. The Civil Rights Bill that was passed in 1964 and the ones that have passed since then succeeded because black folks had allies in their fight. We had strong church groups, liberal Whites, as well as people in the labor movement who were sympathetic to our struggles. Black separatism is an enemy of black political power, and this is a lesson that Blacks in every community, north and south, east and west, must learn.

It is necessary for A.M.E. preachers and preachers in general in local situations to support each other in civil rights activities. The support should take the place of jealousies, criticisms and the knocking of the program simply because someone started what appears to be feasible. The idea of, *"Get with it if it seems workable and feasible and is designed to help our people"* would seem to be the appropriate step on the part of all preachers.

It is felt by some that in each church there should be a social community concerns committee. This committee should study social problems of the community and from time to time report to the church what is taking place in the community. This committee, if called upon to report from time to time, will encourage social awareness among members.

While it is not possible for me to suggest any specific plans of operation, it would seem that local churches need to watch the program of integration as it proceeds. In some communities, Negro teachers have lost their jobs, principals are being displaced unduly, and community consciousness or even community action may be necessary on the local level to offset these practices.

Anyone familiar with today's reality will testify that police brutality is a fact. How far the local leadership may go in attempting to alleviate this prevalent practice must be determined by local situations and conditions.

The handwriting is already on the wall, and America herself shall never be free until it frees the Negro from every practice which denies him full and equal participation in all phases of American citizenship.

Here's some of what still needs to be done:

** We need to get the millions of Blacks who are not registered, for whatever reason, to do so by upcoming elections.

206

Those who are turning eighteen need to be reminded to become registered. We must be ready for elections on all levels of government.

** We need to keep our armor on, because racism and segregation are not dead in America. They are very much alive. Dr. King once said that "Old Man Segregation is dead, and the only thing left is how expensive the segregationist is going to make his funeral." Well, Old Man Segregationist must have nine lives, or he has some bad brothers, because every now and then some hate group will rise up—for example, the "rebel flag" group, the Klu Klux Klan, et cetera. What it took to get us to this point, it will take that and more to keep us here, because there are forces right now trying very hard to take back every gain the Negro has made. I hear white folks talking about, "I'm a conservative," which is a new way of saying segregationist. They would like to preserve the Old Southern Way.

** We need to move up in the corporate world. We have the right to vote and have elected a few Mayors, Representatives, Senators, et cetera. We got a few folks inside the door, for showcase and tokenism, but very, very few are up where the decisions are made. It seems that everybody that comes to this country can get ahead in the corporate world except the Negro. Let us not stop until we have reached our goal in the corporate world.

** Heads up and eyes open for election reform. The Congress and the President have been discussing it. We need election reform so that we won't have a repeat of the election in 2000, which was a disgrace. President George W. Bush, it has been alleged, was selected by the Supreme Court and not elected by the people.

As part of the reform process, there needs to be an Amendment that prohibits a person, once he or she is elected by a party, from changing parties. Once elected, the individual shall remain with the party until his or her term expires. Alternatively, the person can resign and run for office representing the party they are switching to. There has been too much switching after the people of a party worked to get a politician elected.

** We must learn to live together here on the Planet Earth. Although Blacks and Whites came over here in different ships, we are in the same boat now. What affects one will affect us all. Tears are colorless, pains are color blind. We must learn to live together as sisters and brothers or we will die as fools. We cannot think of living separately here and together in God's heaven. It doesn't work that way.

** An all-out effort should be made to stop the Black-on-Black killing in the black community, or in any community. The move should be on to curb teenage pregnancy, where babies are having babies. They are not able to take care of themselves; how can they take care of a baby? This speaks to the strength of the race and its moral fabric. Too many of our promising young men are in prisons. We need programs of prevention for our boys and girls. We need to move to get dope peddlers off our doorsteps and out of our communities. If everyone worked to clean up their streets in their communities, we would have good communities.

** Black folks need to move back to the church, the bridge that brought us out of the land of Egypt and the house of bondage. The old saying is, *"Never burn the bridge that brought you safely across."* At times the church was the only thing that we could call our own, and no one could stop us from meeting in it. For Christ's sake, let us not lose the church. The church must be concerned about the whole family and their well-being, "deadbeat dads," and the support they are giving to the family.

The church is concerned about the total man. Let the church never forget its mission and purpose, which is to seek out and save the lost and serve the needy through a program of: (1) preaching the gospel, (2) feeding the hungry, (3) clothing the naked, (4) housing the homeless, (5) cheering the fallen, (6) providing jobs for the jobless, (7) administering to the needs of those in prisons, nursing homes, asylums and mental institutions, senior citizens' homes, caring for the sick, the shut-ins, the mentally and socially disturbed, and (8) encouraging thrift and economic advancement. This should be a constant effort!

** Let us continue to move in Higher Education. "A mind is still a terrible thing to waste." "How do we waste a mind? Sometimes through carelessness, laziness, playfulness, et cetera. We need to teach our children the importance of studying, and making good grades. Have them cut off the TV, radio, telephone, and so on and spend some quality time studying and you will see the difference in the grades. There was a time in the history of this country, when it was illegal to teach Negroes how to read and write. Many were caught teaching them, and were taken out and hanged. But we can teach them now without fear of reprisal. One of the reasons we are where we are today is because of the educated geniuses of the past. So let us fight on till victory is won!

** Black folks need to stop selling land that their foreparents sweated for and left to them as an inheritance. In too many instances, they give the land away because the sale price is so cheap. Remember, God is not going to make any more land, so hold on to what you have and be sure to pay the tax on it. In 1972, when I was attending the Urban Training Center in Chicago, Illinois, it was reported that black folks owned more than sixteen million acres of land in America. In 2001, they own fewer than twelve million acres. So we can see the need to hold on to your land. Land very seldom depreciates.

BIBLIOGRAPHY

Black Protest by New York Press.

Responsible Preaching by William A. Jones.

Black Heritage Calendar 1988.

The World Book Encyclopedia Volume 2, B. Volume 10 J-K,
Volume N-O: Volume 7 - G. Volume 13, Volume 18 , U, V.

The A.M.E. Church and the Current Negro Revolt Published
by A.M.E. Sunday school union, Nashville, Tennessee.

A Study of Black Participation by Negroes in the Electoral
and Political Processes in Ten Southern States Since the
Passage of the Voting Right Act in 1965.

The A.M.E. Review Published by the A.M.E. Sunday School
Union, Nashville, Tennessee.

The Selma *Times Journal* Newspaper, Selma, Alabama.

Black in Selma By J. L. Chestnut.

While We Can't Wait by Martin Luther King, Jr.

King James Version of the *Bible*.